Best Wishes
Bettie Aycock

Glen-Ella Springs

RECIPES AND REMEMBRANCES

Barrie Aycock

Cover and illustrations by John Kollock
Photographs by Barrie Aycock and Chip Simone

First Edition
First Printing, October 1997
Copyright © 1997 Glen-Ella Springs, Inc.
7,000 copies

This book is a collection of our favorite recipes,
which are not necessarily original recipes.

Library of Congress Catalog number: 97-74770
ISBN: 0-9659404-0-3

Edited by Barrie Aycock

Designed and manufactured in the
United States of America by Favorite Recipes® Press
an imprint of

RP

2451 Atrium Way, Nashville, Tennessee 37214
1-800-358-0560

Cover and Illustrations by John Kollock
Photography by Barrie Aycock and Chip Simone

For reservations and information about Glen-Ella Springs Inn
please call 706-754-7295 or write Glen-Ella Springs Inn
1789 Bear Gap Road
Clarkesville, Georgia 30523
Email: info@glenella.com
Visit us on the world wide web at www.glenella.com

Dedication

This book is dedicated to my family.
Bobby who has been my mate
and best friend for 34 years plus a few.
Our daughter Amy who has blessed us by marrying a
dear kind person named Churchill, moving back to Georgia
from California and giving us Cameron Blatnik, our first grandchild.
Our son Rob who has followed in his parents' footsteps
in more ways than one, but especially in marrying Brandy
after a courtship that lasted as long as his parents' did.
They gave us our granddaughter, Addie,
six months after our grandson was born.

This isn't always an easy business
and I tend to get involved in too many things at one time.
I want to do it all, my way, and I know that frustrates others at times.
Together we have made a special place and it could not have
happened without everybody's help and endless patience
with me and my eccentricities.

Contents

✽ Indicates recipes which are lighter fare.

About the Inn

GLEN-ELLA SPRINGS is a full-service country inn in the Northeast Georgia mountains 90 miles north of Atlanta in the northeast corner of the state about 20 miles south of the North Carolina line and about 20 miles west of the South Carolina line. A four-lane highway now connects us with metropolitan Atlanta, making the drive just over an hour.

The property consists of 18 acres of meadow with herb, perennial and vegetable gardens; a 20x40-foot swimming pool and sun deck; and a mountain stream and one of the original mineral springs which has been partially restored.

The inn is almost surrounded by the Chatta-hoochee National Forest. There are state parks in the area with hiking trails, water falls, and lakes. There are also charming historic villages, interesting build-ings, antiques, golf, rafting and horseback riding nearby, but many of our guests enjoy most just rocking

on the porch and listening to the birds sing.

Glen-Ella Springs is a favorite spot for corporate meetings, which keep us busy during mid-week, while the weekends are normally reserved for leisure travellers. A large modern conference room is located on the lower level of the innkeepers' house, and five acres of land across the creek is used in corporate team-building programs. The inn is a favorite spot for spring and early summer weddings.

Our restoration efforts won awards from the Georgia Trust for Historic Preservation and the building was placed on the National Register of Historic Places even though we made some minor changes to the exterior. We retained the original heart pine panelling throughout the building, but much of it has been whitewashed to brighten the guest rooms.

Glen-Ella Springs is proud to be a member of the Independent Innkeepers' Association, an international association of over 300 of the finest inns in North America. These inns are chosen very carefully and have to meet and maintain rigorous standards of hospitality and cleanliness. A guidebook of member inns is given free of charge to every inn guest.

History of Glen-Ella Springs

Glen-Ella Springs was named for Glen and Ella Davidson who built a three-room residence on the property around 1875 and added guest accommodations around 1890. The land was part of 600 acres granted to Glen Davidson's father after the Cherokee Indians were moved from this part of Georgia. Glen and Ella's property was about 360 acres.

An early photograph of the building shows two separate structures. The main structure is where the current lobby and dining room are, and must have been Glen and Ella's original residence. The second structure containing the original guest quarters was incorporated into a larger addition around 1900 when the building was enlarged to its current size.

The addition of guest rooms was certainly prompted by the arrival of the railroad into the Tallulah Falls area in 1882. The nearest station was in Turnerville, two and one-half miles from the inn. Guests came from the lowlands of Georgia and South Carolina to escape the summer's heat and yellow fever, and to "take the waters" at the mineral springs on the property. There probably wasn't much to do except eat and sleep, and rock on the porch.

Nearby Tallulah Falls was also a nationally known attraction. Visitors were met at the Turnerville railroad station and transported to the inn by means of surrey and covered wagon for the

luggage. The surrey remained on Glen-Ella's front porch until the 1950s but, unfortunately for us, had disappeared before we came into the picture.

The accommodations were not luxurious. There was no indoor plumbing, just a three-holer in the backyard. All the rooms had interior windows opening into each other, I suppose for air circulation, so there wasn't much privacy.

There was a gravity-flow water system which brought water from across Panther Creek into the kitchen and then flowed out of the kitchen into the pig pens. The hollowed out wooden water pipes were still in the kitchen when we purchased the building.

Glen and Ella had five children, two sons and three daughters. Very little is known about the two sons. One of them is reported to have returned shell-shocked from World War I. We're told that he was so fat he was unable to fit in the family's new Model A and had to continue to drive the surrey. The other son moved to the Northwest and hasn't been heard from since.

Of the three daughters, only one ever married. Her name was Drucilla. She married a McClure, and all the direct descendants we know about are McClures. Mary was the oldest daughter. She took over the operation of the inn in 1914 after the death of her parents. Another daughter named Ida developed some type of mental illness in her early twenties and moved back and forth between here and the state hospital in Milledgeville. I believe she lived longer than any of the others. After Mary died in 1942, her sister Naomi came back to Georgia from California and lived here until she died in the early sixties. We have an *Atlanta-Journal Constitution* interview with Naomi dated September 7, 1958, in which she was quoted as saying the hotel once contained 46 rooms — 40 of them bedrooms. No way! There were only 27. Don't believe everything you read in the newspaper.

After the falls were dammed, the area lost its attraction to tourists and the family began raising produce and dairy products to help feed the large work camps which housed those who were building the dam and series of lakes, including Rabun, Burton and Seed, that were made by the damming of the Tallulah River. This was actually the first public works project in the United States, several years before WPA.

By 1915 there were only a few guests coming to Glen-Ella Springs. Glen and Ella both died around that time. Mary, the eldest daughter, continued to live here with Ida. We have had two visitors who remembered being here as a guest. Both of them were small children at the time, so their memories were somewhat vague, but we have collected a few tales from local sources and former guests. We even had Mr. Marion McClure, the grandson of Glen and Ella, as an overnight guest. He was in his nineties at the time, and has since died. When we saw him, his memory was excellent and he was able to give us much valuable information.

One story we were told was that Mary, the daughter, received word that a group who was coming to stay would like to have chicken livers for their dinner. She was most upset that she had to kill chickens just for the livers, so she charged them for the whole chickens.

The local folks also say Miss Mary hid her money outside in a fruit jar. She would disappear to the backyard and reappear with the money. Nobody ever knew where she hid it. One of the Davidson descendants told me there was a local scandal about one of the relatives running out of Mary's room with a sack of money when Mary was on her deathbed. The story is that the other relatives called the sheriff and she was arrested, they got the money back and this lady died soon after with a strange unexplained illness. I honestly do not know if there is a word of truth in this tale or not, but every time I dig in the backyard, I'm on the lookout for some buried treasure.

In 1962 the property was sold for $5,000 to Reverend A. A. Phillips, who had been the family's pastor at the Methodist church in Tallulah Falls. He operated the place as a boys' home known as Boys Mountain Ranch between 1962 and 1965. Miss Naomi continued to live here for about a year after the boys' home was opened.

About 1965 Reverend Phillips landed in the hospital with a heart attack. The church obviously didn't have much hope for his recovery because they sold the property while he was in the hospital. Twenty years later in 1985, Bobby and I located Reverend Phillips and his new

bride in Augusta and he was still mad about the church selling his boys' home.

The first summer we were open, one of the boys who had lived at the boys' home came by with his family. He was quite surprised and delighted to find that it not only was still standing but looked much better than it had when he had lived here. I asked him what it had been like in this old building with no plumbing. He described it rather positively, saying they had a pretty good time.

The next owners were Mr. and Mrs. J. C. Thompson from Gainesville, Georgia. They used this place as a summer home and actually were responsible for giving the building its first coat of paint. In 1985, Don Newsome bought the property, which was still 365 acres. He developed second-home sites on the portion across Bear Gap Road. A year later we purchased 18 acres containing the inn from Mr. Newsome. The remaining 100 or so acres behind the inn (our property is bordered by Panther Creek), are also being developed by Mr. Newsome as second-home sites.

Don Newsome was responsible for gathering much of the information we have about the family. After he purchased the property, he made a great effort to interview all the Davidson family still in the area, and actually recorded much that they told him on tape.

Introduction

This is my second Glen-Ella Springs cookbook. The first one was published in 1992 after five years at the inn. It contained only sixty-two pages. Half was narrative about the history of the inn and its innkeepers and half was recipes. At this writing, there are still a few hundred copies left of the old one if anybody's interested. Since then we have developed and collected many new and wonderful recipes, and in celebration of our tenth anniversary as innkeepers of Glen-Ella Springs, I decided it was time for a second and somewhat larger edition. I enjoy writing recipes. I must say also that computers make the job much easier than it used to be.

For those who don't already know us, Bobby and I moved to this area from Atlanta in 1987 after raising two children who now are living here in Habersham County with their families, and at least one member of both families works for us. Bobby was in the construction business and I was 45 years old and didn't know what I wanted to be when I grew up! My first love and favorite hobby had always been good food—eating, cooking and just talking about it makes me happy. I wanted a business that involved food, and Bobby wanted to get out of Atlanta and out of the construction business.

One day in June of 1986 we were at our weekend cabin on Lake Rabun when some friends mentioned that the old hotel on Bear Gap Road was for sale and they knew some people who were thinking about buying and

renovating the building. "What old hotel?" we asked, and learned that the falling-down structure on that gorgeous piece of property on the road which led to the lake had at one time been a hotel. We had passed the building hundreds of times and admired the view of the meadow, but never once had dreamed that the awful looking old building had once been a hotel.

We were hooked from that point on—this was the answer to our dream. Never mind that the place looked like a strong wind would blow it away, or that it was two and one-half miles down a dirt road in the middle of nowhere, or that we had no idea how to run an inn, much less a restaurant. Not to mention that the building had not been seriously inhabited in 50 years and had no plumbing or electricity. We felt from that first moment that this was what we had been looking for—and it was.

After many months of investigation, we purchased the property, found a contractor, sold our house in Atlanta and the one at the lake, borrowed as much money as the local bank would lend us and began renovations in December of 1986.

In June of 1987 we moved here, leaving both children in Atlanta. Our son was finishing his last year of high school and didn't want to move, so he stayed behind with friends. Our daughter was out of school and living on her own. The part of the building which contained the dining room and two upstairs suites was livable, so we moved in there and stored the rest of our belongings in a prefab building behind the Turnerville General Store. Had we known it would be more than a year before we would have a closet again, we might have had second thoughts, but we were excited and positive about our new future.

I had done a brief stint as a prep cook in a well known Atlanta restaurant, thanks to my friend Elise who got me the job, so I knew a little bit about how to operate a restaurant, but not much. We knew absolutely nothing about running an inn except that you had to make beds, clean toilets and cook breakfast just

like you did at home—what could be hard about that? Of course, we didn't have sixteen bedrooms and bathrooms at home. We actually managed fairly well. We found some wonderful employees who lived nearby, and we weren't very busy at the inn that first summer, so we had time to learn as we went.

The restaurant was another story. We were packed from the very beginning. There had never been a fine dining restaurant in the area, and all the summer people from the nearby lakes flocked to our doors. We had no idea how to take reservations, so we just told everybody to come whenever they wanted to. It was chaos! Bobby remembers one Saturday night when he had a table of twelve seated in the dining room, another table of twelve waiting in the lobby and another table of twelve waiting outside—and only one table where that many people could sit at one time. The first cook I hired never darkened the door. I did it myself the first month with the help of some wonderful friends and family until we found someone.

Joe Cukla, a student at Piedmont College, was our first chef. I can't believe how little we paid him and how hard he worked. He stayed with us for two years and was succeeded by another and another about every two years. Last June, Jeff McKenna became our current chef. Jeff is a graduate of Johnson and Wales in Charleston, South Carolina, and came here from another inn and

restaurant in Key West, Florida. This spring we have Chris Secrest as our first professionally trained sous-chef and he also came from Johnson and Wales. I can't believe how much we have to pay them, but they still work hard! Jeff and his wife, who is our pastry chef, have just bought a house nearby, so we're hoping they'll be here for a while.

We still retain a few of the items from our original menu. It's hard to keep them the same with different chefs but we try our best. Of course, we've added and changed many things in the dining room, including — but not limited to — the menu. We took out tables and chairs for one thing, so we don't serve nearly as many in the dining room as we did in the beginning. Now our first priority is our overnight guests although we do serve dinner to others when space is available. We have modernized the kitchen, although we still have a 100-year-old wood floor which is so unlevel that if you drop something and it rolls, you may never find it again.

We continue to upgrade the furnishings and accessories in the rooms every year, and we've done extensive work on the gardens with a succession of gardeners — not unlike the chef situation. Now we have three different people besides me who help with the garden in varying degrees. Doris has the local garden center down on the highway. She sells us plants and tends to the flowers in the summer. Brad is a young longtime family friend who is a horticulturist at the Atlanta History Center. He advises me on design and native plant materials. And Tim, who does everything having to do with maintenance around here, takes care of our summer vegetable garden. This year he has germinated all our vegetables and annuals from seed and, if the deer don't eat them all, we should have wonderful flowers and vegetables this summer.

The front desk has also seen many changes. Susan Keefer is enjoying her first summer as our front desk manager and coping very well. The guests enjoy her friendly smile and helpful manner. Our loyal housekeeping staff is headed by Ruth Matheson who has been with us for many years and who is my right arm. I tell her if she ever leaves, I'm going with her. Her cheerful manner, wonderful attitude and attention to

detail are exceptional. Diane Chapman, our other full-time house-keeper, is also as loyal and faithful as anyone could ask. God bless housekeepers!

Many of our wait staff come and go, but a few of them have been with us for a long time. Churchill, our son-in-law, is our mainstay at night in the dining room. Ann helps me with breakfast on the weekends and is here often at night also when she's not taking care of a house full of grandchildren. Our longtime dining room employee, Teresa, is staying at home more these days with her teenagers, but she still helps us out when we need her. Kelley, Sharon and others are here when we're busy, and we appreciate their loyalty.

Our son Rob is our conference coordinator. His wife Brandy cooks break-fast for our conference groups with the help of Lou, who is also our baker. Brandy and Rob have a baby daughter named Addie who spends a lot of time here also and gives her grandfather another job as number-one babysitter. Addie at this writing is not mobile yet, so she's still allowed in the inn anytime, while our grandson Cameron, who belongs to Amy and Churchill and is now fourteen months old and into everything, has to restrict his inn visits to the times when we're not busy.

We are constantly changing things around to be more efficient. This spring Rob moved his office to the space just off the lobby which was added a few years ago as my office and then became the gift shop. I now have as my office the entire space which was built as the gift shop and which Rob and I shared. Our gift shop has now shrunk to the étagère beside the front desk with a few things on the bookcase by the fireplace. So you see how things change through the years. Bobby and I look forward to the time when Rob and Brandy will take over as innkeepers and move into our house, and we'll move to the back of the property and only come to the inn to check up on everybody. That won't happen for many years, but it's a good feeling to know at least for now that our family wants to continue our tradition here at Glen-Ella Springs.

Barrie's Garden

Food at the Inn

Our menu changes daily, but some items on our menu have been with us since we opened, like Trout Pecan and Key Lime Pie. They're still popular so we keep them around. When new chefs come they bring a new style and new ways of doing things. Many longtime customers request some of the things we used to serve which our new chefs either didn't want to continue or were replaced with new things and forgotten over time.

I think our food has stayed consistently good. I am not in the kitchen at night any more. I never was any good at line cooking and I think if you are going to hire professional chefs, you need to give them the authority to do their job as they are trained to do. I do stay very involved in the kitchen on a daily basis however. I sample almost every new dish we prepare and I am the chefs' worst and best critic. I also plan most of our banquet and wedding menus, and I'm constantly nagging the staff about keeping the kitchen neat and clean.

My personal food philosophy is simple. I believe every ingredient should be the best quality available, and my favorite foods are those simple things like a perfectly ripe tomato or a freshly caught fish which need almost nothing to enhance their wonderful flavor. I don't like dried herbs as a general rule, but there are some exceptions as you will see. We grow many fresh herbs in our garden in the summer and use them in abundance.

You won't get very far with these recipes if you don't own a food processor and a wire whisk. You'll also need some Dijon mustard and some fairly good olive oil. I prefer unsalted butter; the salt is added as a preservative and the flavor of unsalted butter is much better. Many of the recipes from the inn contain heavy cream. It makes almost anything taste better. You can usually substitute half-and-half or milk, but your results won't be quite the same. You'll find a number of recipes using black-eyed peas. It's a "southern thing" and they are so handy and versatile.

Some of the recipes in this book are original, but not very many. Most of them came from friends or other cookbooks. I have tried to give credit for the origin when I remembered where it came from, but many times I don't. All I can say is that they are all favorites of mine or of friends of mine. Some of these recipes we prepare regularly in the kitchen but in larger quantities. The computer is wonderful for helping to scale recipes up and down and I have tried to test most of them in the smaller quantities, but if you have a question about any recipe in the book, call me at the inn (706-754-7295) and I'll try to answer it for you.

Appetizers

Basil Dip for Artichokes and Other Vegetables

—◈◈◈—

1/4	cup lemon juice
1/2	cup fresh basil leaves, tightly packed
1/4	cup parsley
1/2	teaspoon salt
1	clove garlic
1/4	teaspoon dry mustard
1	cup mayonnaise

❧ Combine all ingredients except mayonnaise in a food processor or blender. Process until smooth.

❧ Transfer to a small bowl and stir in mayonnaise. Taste and correct seasonings. (If too tart add a little milk.) Chill until ready to serve.

❧ Serve as a dip with steamed artichokes or any raw or lightly steamed vegetables.

❧ Will keep in refrigerator for at least a week.

YIELD: 32 (1-TABLESPOON) SERVINGS

Black-Eyed Pea Salsa*

————— ⌒⌒⌒ —————

1	(16-ounce) package frozen black-eyed peas
1	teaspoon salt
1/2	teaspoon ground red pepper
1	bay leaf
2	cups boiling water
1 1/2	cups Roma tomatoes
1 1/2	tablespoons seeded and finely chopped jalapeño pepper
2	tablespoons chopped fresh cilantro leaves or 1 tablespoon dried
1	tablespoon fresh lime juice
3	tablespoons minced green onions
1/2	teaspoon salt

2➤ Cook black-eyed peas with salt, red pepper and bay leaf in boiling water just until tender.

2➤ Core tomatoes and squeeze to remove juice and most of the seeds. Cut in 1/4-inch dice.

2➤ Mix tomatoes and remaining ingredients in a bowl. Add the peas and mix well. Taste and adjust seasonings.

2➤ Serve with tortilla chips. Will keep several days refrigerated.

YIELD: 12 SERVINGS OR 4 CUPS

Sun-Dried Tomato Pesto

—⟨ℴℴℴ⟩—

In adding oil to pesto, I use just enough to make a smooth paste. The amounts given are approximate. Also I use a peanut or vegetable oil but olive oil may be used as well—just always make sure your olive oil is fresh and of top quality.

½	cup sun-dried tomatoes (not packed in oil)
¼	cup white wine (optional)
1	clove (or more) garlic
1	tablespoon tomato paste
¼	cup (or more) vegetable oil
¼	cup finely grated Parmesan cheese
	Salt and pepper to taste

❧ Chop tomatoes if they are whole. Combine tomatoes, wine and enough water to cover in a bowl. Soak the tomatoes for 30 minutes or until soft. Drain and squeeze juice from tomatoes, reserving liquid.

❧ Combine tomatoes, garlic, tomato paste, oil and cheese in food processor. Process until smooth. Add salt and pepper if needed. Remove from processor and thin if desired with some of the reserved soaking liquid.

❧ If you are making the Cream Cheese and Pesto Mold (page 28), it helps to add some extra liquid to the Tomato Pesto so it is easier to spread in a thin layer over the other ingredients.

YIELD: 1 SERVING

Yogurt Cheese and Herbed Yogurt Cheese*

Use as a base to make spreads, dips, low-fat desserts, cheese balls and sauces. It is also a good substitute for sour cream or crème fraîche. Use a dollop of yogurt cheese to top soups and omelets instead of sour cream.

2	cups nonfat plain yogurt
1	tablespoon minced green onions
1	tablespoon minced fresh parsley
1	tablespoon minced fresh basil or dill
1	teaspoon finely minced garlic
	Salt and freshly ground pepper to taste

- Spoon the yogurt into a colander or strainer lined with a porus material (several layers of cheesecloth, a cotton kitchen towel or a cloth napkin).
- Put the colander over a bowl to collect the excess moisture. Refrigerate for 5 hours or overnight.
- The longer you strain the yogurt, the thicker it will become. Two cups of yogurt will make ¾ cup yogurt cheese.
- **Herbed Yogurt Cheese:** Mix cheese made from 2 cups yogurt with remaining ingredients. Season to taste. Serve with pita chips, etc.

YIELD: 8 SERVINGS

Baked Brie with Warm Spicy Peach Coulis

1	(15-ounce) brie wheel
1	teaspoon cinnamon
1	package puff pastry (available in grocery store)
12	ounces fresh peaches, peeled, chopped
1/4	cup sugar
2	quarts water
1	teaspoon cayenne pepper
2	shakes Tabasco sauce

- Sprinkle brie with cinnamon.
- Wrap completely in puff pastry. Place on greased baking pan.
- Bake in 350-degree oven for 10 minutes or until brown.
- Cook peaches with sugar and water in a saucepan until very tender. Drain, reserving liquid.
- Purée peaches in blender or food processor.
- Add enough reserved liquid to peaches to get a smooth pourable consistency.
- Season with pepper and Tabasco sauce.
- Pour peach coulis onto a serving plate. Place the pastry wrapped brie on the coulis just before serving.

YIELD: 12 SERVINGS

Bleu Cheese Pesto Spread

Basil pesto can be purchased in most gourmet food stores or can be made in a food processor from fresh basil, olive oil, Parmesan cheese and nuts. Other pestos such as Basil-Spinach Pesto (page 26) or Sun-Dried Tomato Pesto (page 22) can be used instead of the basil pesto.

> 8 *ounces cream cheese, softened*
> 2 *ounces (or more) bleu cheese,*
>   *crumbled, softened*
> 1 *ounce (or more to taste) basil pesto*
>   *(see headnote)*

❧ Combine cream cheese and bleu cheese with pesto and mix well in food processor or by hand.

YIELD: 16 SERVINGS

Basil

Basil-Spinach Pesto

This is the pesto I developed to use in our Cream Cheese Pesto Mold (page 28). The addition of spinach assures that the pesto remains a bright, pretty green color. This pesto is also good tossed with pasta, or in any other way you would use a traditional basil pesto. The basil flavor is less intense, which is preferable for many purposes. You can use this same basic recipe leaving out the spinach for a traditional Basil Pesto.

½	cup chopped walnuts or whole pine nuts
1	(10-ounce) package frozen chopped spinach, squeezed dry
1½	cups fresh basil leaves, loosely packed (or use up to ¾ cup fresh parsley in place of some of the basil)
2	cloves (or more) fresh garlic, peeled
1	cup (or more) vegetable oil
1½	cups finely grated Parmesan cheese
¼	teaspoon salt
¼	teaspoon black pepper

≈ Roast nuts in a 375-degree oven for about 5 minutes or just until beginning to color; cool.

≈ Place spinach, basil and garlic in a food processor. With motor running slowly pour in oil and process until well blended, adding a little more oil if needed to make a smooth paste. Add nuts, cheese, salt and pepper and process until mixture is smooth. Taste and add more seasoning if desired. Refrigerate up to 3 days, or freeze. Try freezing any leftover pesto in ice cube trays, then pop them out into a zip-lock bag for use as needed in small portions.

≈ Pesto cubes are great as a quick pasta sauce. Stir in pesto cubes with some heavy cream or a light bechamel sauce. Toss with pasta, Parmesan cheese and freshly ground pepper. Add pesto cubes to vegetable soup; spread on rounds of toasted bread for a typical Italian snack; mix with cream cheese and a little bleu cheese and spread on crackers.

YIELD: 12 SERVINGS

Pea Pâté

—⟋⟍⟋⟍⟋—

1	(16-ounce) package frozen crowder or black-eyed peas
½	teaspoon salt
2	teaspoons olive oil
15	large fresh basil leaves
½	cup fresh parsley, stems removed
1	cup chopped pecans
2	cloves garlic, quartered
½	cup freshly grated Parmesan cheese
1	cup (or less) olive oil

- Cook the frozen peas with salt and 2 teaspoons olive oil in a saucepan until soft but not mushy. Reserve ¾ cup of the peas.
- Put remaining peas in bowl of food processor with metal blade. Add basil, parsley, pecans, garlic and Parmesan. Process briefly until blended.
- Add olive oil slowly in a steady stream, processing constantly until mixture is smooth and the consistency of a pâté. You may not need all the oil.
- Add in the reserved peas and blend very briefly so some are still mostly whole.
- This clues the guests to the fact that this pâté is made with vegetables, not liver!
- Serve with stoned wheat crackers.

YIELD: 32 SERVINGS

Cream Cheese and Pesto Mold

—⟨∂⟩∂∂⟨∂⟩—

½   cup Sun-Dried Tomato Pesto
       (page 22)
1   recipe Basil-Spinach Pesto (page 26)
12   ounces cream cheese, softened
6   ounces crumbled bleu cheese, softened

✍ Use a 6-inch springform pan or any other 4-cup mold. Line mold with plastic wrap, allowing enough extra on sides to cover top of mold when finished. This makes unmolding much easier.

✍ Make Sun-Dried Tomato Pesto.

✍ Make Basil-Spinach Pesto.

✍ Combine the cream cheese and the bleu cheese in a bowl and mix well.

✍ Place a layer (about 1 cup) of cheese mixture in a mold and using wet fingers spread to cover bottom.

✍ Cover with a layer (about ¾ cup) of Basil-Spinach Pesto, and a thin layer (¼ cup) of Sun-Dried Tomato Pesto.

✍ Repeat with another layer of half the remaining cheese mixture, the 2 pestos and top with remaining cheese mixture. Cover and refrigerate overnight.

✍ Several hours before serving, remove cheese from mold. If mold is still soft, you can place in freezer for about 30 minutes before serving.

✍ Cut cheese into 4 wedges if desired, arrange on platter, garnish with fresh basil sprigs and chopped parsley and serve as a spread with plain crackers or toasted French bread rounds. Leftover wedges can be frozen.

YIELD: 12 SERVINGS

Marinated Goat Cheese

———

This idea came from my friend Elise (Griffin) Hughes who helped design our original menu. She now has a very successful catering business, "It's Your Party," in Atlanta. The amounts given here are approximate. Use your own judgement and vary ingredients to suit your taste. If there's any left over, this is also wonderful tossed with pasta for a quick dinner.

2	(5-ounce) packages good quality goat cheese
1/2	teaspoon coarsely ground black pepper
1/2	teaspoon dried red pepper flakes
1/2	teaspoon chopped garlic
3	tablespoons thinly sliced canned or fresh-roasted red peppers
2	tablespoons sun-dried tomatoes, cut in small strips
4	Calamata olives, pitted, sliced
1/2	cup sliced red or Vidalia onion
1	tablespoon chopped fresh herbs
3/4	cup good quality olive oil

- Slice cold goat cheese into rounds about 1 inch thick and place in shallow dish just large enough for slices to fit comfortably.
- Sprinkle cheese with black pepper and red pepper flakes.
- Top each round equally with garlic, red peppers, sun-dried tomatoes, olives, onion and herbs.
- Pour olive oil over to barely cover. Refrigerate 1 to 2 days before serving.
- Will keep practically forever—at least a week—and gets better the longer it sits.
- Serve with crackers or toast rounds.

YIELD: 8 SERVINGS

Goat Cheese and Roasted Garlic Soufflés with Tomato-Basil Sauce

This is one of my favorite appetizers. It has been a favorite at our garlic lovers' dinners and other special occasions. The original recipe came from a class Elizabeth Terry demonstrated at the AIWF Southern Food Festival in Atlanta in '89 or '90. I have changed it some over the years, but not a lot. The great thing about this dish is that it is a make-ahead soufflé! You can even make it the day before, but they will look better if they are served the same day you make them.

3	large whole heads garlic, not peeled
¾	cup white wine
2	tablespoons good quality olive oil
2	tablespoons butter
2	tablespoons all-purpose flour
1	cup milk
10	ounces goat cheese, crumbled
4	large eggs, separated
⅓	cup finely grated Parmesan or Romano cheese
½	small bunch fresh basil, stems removed
	Tomato-Basil Sauce

➣ Cut the top off each head of garlic with a sharp knife, just barely exposing the garlic buds. Place the garlic heads, cut side up in a garlic roaster or small ceramic dish. Drizzle with the wine and olive oil. Roast, covered with a lid or foil, at 350 degrees for 45 minutes to 1 hour or until the garlic heads are soft. Cool and squeeze the garlic into a small bowl, extracting as much as possible. Discard skins.

➣ Melt 2 tablespoons of butter in a nonstick skillet. Stir in the flour until smooth. Add the roasted garlic and mix well. Cook over low heat for 2 minutes, stirring constantly. Whisk in the milk. Bring to a boil, cooking until thickened and stirring constantly. Remove from the heat and whisk in the goat cheese. Cool slightly. Whisk in the egg yolks.

⁊➤ Beat the egg whites in a mixer bowl until stiff but not dry. Fold into the soufflé mixture. Divide evenly among 6 greased muffin cups or custard cups, filling about ⅔ full. Place in a water bath.

⁊➤ Bake at 350 degrees for 20 to 30 minutes or until brown on top and cooked all the way through. Test by inserting a knife in the center; it should come out clean. Remove from the oven. When cool enough to handle, invert onto a baking sheet. Refrigerate if not serving within an hour or two.

⁊➤ Just before serving, preheat the oven to 450 degrees. Sprinkle the Parmesan cheese over the soufflés. Bake at 450 degrees for 5 to 10 minutes or until warm and slightly brown on top. Shred the basil leaves into julienne strips with a sharp knife.

⁊➤ Place the soufflés on serving dishes. Top with Tomato-Basil Sauce and garnish with the fresh basil strips.

YIELD: 6 SERVINGS

Tomato-Basil Sauce

1	clove of garlic, minced
2	tablespoons good quality olive oil
1	(28-ounce) can Italian tomatoes, crushed
¼	teaspoon salt
½	teaspoon black pepper
½	small bunch fresh basil, stems removed

⁊➤ Sauté the garlic in the olive oil in a saucepan. Add the undrained tomatoes, salt and pepper.

⁊➤ Simmer over low heat for about 20 minutes or until slightly thickened, stirring frequently. Set aside until ready to use. Refrigerate if more than an hour or two.

⁊➤ Heat the sauce just before serving. Shred the basil leaves into julienne strips with a sharp knife. Stir into the hot sauce.

Chicken Livers with Mushrooms, Country Ham and Marsala

These were on our original menu when we opened ten years ago. They were another of Elise's creations, and were extremely popular with many of our guests. The problem was that not enough of our guests ordered them on a regular basis. We were always having to throw half of the livers away, plus cooking them is somewhat dangerous as they will pop in the pan and burn your arm in a second. So through the years and a succession of chefs, they were ignored until our current chef who had never even seen the recipe. I doubt they will ever reappear on our menu, so here's the recipe for anyone who is brave enough to try to make them. I am not responsible for any damage caused to flesh by cooking them!

8	ounces chicken livers
	Our Coating Mix (page 138)
1/4	cup peanut or vegetable oil
1/4	cup (1-inch) country ham pieces
1/2	cup mushroom halves
1/4	cup (1/4-inch) onion pieces
1/4	cup sweet Marsala wine
1/2	teaspoon chopped fresh sage

- Blot livers with paper towels and cut any extra-large pieces in half—they should all be about the same size. Coat with Our Coating Mix and shake off excess.
- Heat oil in large nonstick skillet until it is hot. Add chicken livers to the skillet. Sauté over moderately high heat until browned on 1 side.
- Add ham, mushrooms and onions to skillet. Turn chicken livers and continue cooking quickly until they are nicely browned on all sides. Add Marsala—it will flame up, so move out of the way of the flame. Reduce heat and sprinkle sage over chicken livers. Cook another minute or two until liquid is reduced to a glaze. Remove chicken livers from skillet and serve immediately.
- The tricky part of this recipe is to get the oil just hot enough to brown the livers without burning the mushrooms and onions.

YIELD: 2 SERVINGS

Grilled Portobella Mushrooms for Six

If preparing more than one hour before cooking, pour off excess marinade and refrigerate mushrooms until needed. This is our most popular appetizer.

1	pint peanut oil or vegetable oil
1	tablespoon chopped fresh garlic
1	tablespoon dried basil
1	tablespoon dried oregano
1/2	teaspoon liquid smoke flavoring
1	tablespoon salt
1 1/2	teaspoons Worcestershire sauce
6	large portobella mushrooms
1	cup balsamic vinegar
1/4	cup sugar
1/2	cup peanut or vegetable oil
1	tablespoon chopped green onions
2	Roma tomatoes, diced

- Combine the first 7 ingredients with a whisk in a food processor or in large bowl.
- Wipe mushrooms and remove stems; lay flat in shallow pan.
- Pour peanut oil marinade over mushrooms. Marinate, covered, for 30 minutes to 1 hour in the refrigerator. Drain the mushrooms.
- Grill the mushrooms on gas or charcoal grill for about 5 minutes or until tender. Be careful as they will flame up when you place them on the grill.
- Whisk together balsamic vinegar, sugar and 1/2 cup oil for vinaigrette. Add the green onions and tomatoes.
- To serve, place grilled mushrooms on a serving plate. Top with vinaigrette. Garnish with additional green onions if needed.

YIELD: 6 SERVINGS

Vegetable Fritters

1³/₄   cups flour
1   tablespoon baking powder
1   teaspoon sugar
1   teaspoon salt
¹/₄   teaspoon baking soda
¹/₂   teaspoon cayenne pepper
3   eggs
1   cup buttermilk
1   pound carrots, finely grated
¹/₂   jumbo onion, grated
       Oil for deep-frying
       Garlic Parmesan Dipping Sauce
       (page 35)

- Sift together flour, baking powder, sugar, salt, baking soda and cayenne. Add slightly beaten eggs and buttermilk. Mix to a batter.

- Mix vegetables together to make a total of about 5 cups. Add to batter. Drop mixture by tablespoonfuls into 375-degree oil. Cook until golden brown.

- Serve 5 fritters to an order. Serve with Garlic Parmesan Dipping Sauce.

- **Smoked Trout Fritters:** Substitute ¹/₂ pound smoked trout for carrots and onion.

YIELD: 6 SERVINGS

Garlic Parmesan Dipping Sauce

2/3	cup mayonnaise
1/3	cup heavy cream or sour cream
2	teaspoons lemon juice
3	tablespoons Parmesan cheese
2	teaspoons minced fresh garlic
1	tablespoon or more Texas Pete sauce
1	teaspoon dried parsley flakes

⁊➤ Combine mayonnaise, heavy cream or sour cream, lemon juice, Parmesan cheese, garlic, Texas Pete sauce and parsley flakes in a bowl. Whisk until well combined and refrigerate.

⁊➤ May substitute Louisiana-style hot sauce for the Texas Pete sauce. Do not substitute Tabasco sauce.

⁊➤ Serve with Vegetable Fritters (page 34) or any fried foods, or serve as a dip for raw vegetables.

YIELD: 4 SERVINGS

Vegetarian Casserole

A contribution from my friend Sandy who says this is a favorite summer appetizer at her house on Lake Burton. She prepares it early in the day and puts it in the oven before they leave for their late afternoon "cocktail cruise" on the lake. When they return, this wonderful appetizer is ready to serve and enjoy. It would also be a nice addition to any summer cookout.

1	Vidalia onion, sliced
1	red bell pepper, cut into strips
4	tablespoons olive oil
8	(or more) cloves of fresh garlic, finely chopped
1	small eggplant, peeled, sliced into thin rounds
	Salt and pepper to taste
5	tomatoes, sliced
2	large zucchini, sliced
3	tablespoons chopped fresh mild - flavored herbs such as thyme, basil, oregano, parsley, etc.
8	ounces goat cheese, crumbled

- Sauté onion and bell pepper in half the olive oil in a large heavy skillet for about 5 minutes or until tender. Add half the garlic and sauté for 1 minute.

- Spread mixture evenly on the bottom of a 9x13-inch baking dish. Arrange eggplant slices evenly over pepper and onion; season with salt and pepper. Top with a layer of tomatoes and zucchini in alternating rows which overlap each other slightly. Season with salt and pepper. Sprinkle with herbs and remaining garlic. Drizzle with remaining 2 tablespoons olive oil; sprinkle with more salt and pepper.

- Bake at 325 degrees for 1 hour or longer or until vegetables are very tender, basting at least twice with pan juices. Remove from oven and sprinkle crumbled goat cheese over top. Bake for 5 minutes longer or until cheese melts. Serve with chunks of crusty French bread.

YIELD: 10 SERVINGS

Crab Mold

———⟨ʊɾʊɾʊ⟩———

This is another old favorite from Nancy's recipe file. There's nothing new or different here, but it sure is good!

1	envelope unflavored gelatin
1/4	cup cold water
3/4	cup hot water
1	pound fresh or frozen crab meat
1	cup finely chopped celery
4	hard-boiled eggs, peeled, chopped
1	cup mayonnaise
1	teaspoon grated onion
	Juice of 1 lemon
	Cayenne pepper, salt and
	Worcestershire sauce to taste

- ⟨⟩ Soften gelatin in ¼ cup cold water. Stir in ¾ cup very hot water and set aside.
- ⟨⟩ Pick over crab meat and discard any shells. Combine crab meat with celery, eggs, mayonnaise, grated onion and lemon juice. Season to taste with cayenne, salt and Worcestershire sauce.
- ⟨⟩ Stir in gelatin, spoon into desired mold and chill until set.
- ⟨⟩ Unmold and serve whole with crackers as an appetizer or slice and serve on a bed of lettuce as a lovely first course.

YIELD: 4 SERVINGS

Salmon Cured with Tequila and Herbs*

This is another of Sandy's favorites. It is wonderful, and healthy as well. You will need to have plenty of space in your refrigerator to accommodate the salmon while it is curing.

2	pieces cheesecloth large enough to wrap salmon
1	(3-pound) fresh salmon fillet, with skin left on
1/4	cup kosher salt
3	tablespoons sugar
1	tablespoon grated lemon zest
2	teaspoons freshly ground black pepper
1/3	cup coarsely chopped fresh parsley
1/3	cup coarsely chopped fresh dill
1/3	cup good quality tequila
12	Toasted rounds of French bread
1	cup chopped red onion
1	cup capers
3/4	cup Yogurt Cheese (page 23) or sour cream

❧ Place a layer of cheesecloth in a glass dish just large enough to hold the salmon. Lay the salmon on the cheesecloth, skin side down.

❧ Combine the salt, sugar, lemon zest and pepper in a mixing bowl. Sprinkle evenly over the salmon. Scatter the coarsely chopped herbs over the salmon. Place a second piece of cheesecloth over the salmon, gently tucking the edges under the salmon. Sprinkle salmon with the tequila. Turn the salmon skin side up. Cover the pan tightly with plastic wrap, place a smaller pan or tray weighted with bricks or heavy cans on top of the wrapped salmon. Allow the salmon to cure in the refrigerator for 3 days, turning at least once every day.

❧ To serve, remove salmon from pan and gently wipe off the marinade. Turn flesh side up and slice very thinly leaving the skin behind. Serve with toasted rounds of French bread, chopped red onion, capers and Yogurt Cheese or sour cream.

YIELD: 12 SERVINGS

Soups

Barrie's Chili

What could be better on a cold day than a pot of chili. This is my recipe which originally appeared in "Puttin' on the Peachtree" from the Junior League of DeKalb County, which I helped to create in 1979. If you can't find any ground pork, buy some lean boneless pork and grind it in the food processor.

2	pounds ground chuck
1	pound ground pork
3	medium yellow onions, chopped
4	cloves of garlic, chopped
1	tablespoon all-purpose flour
4	tablespoons (or more) chili powder
2	(4-ounce) cans chopped green chiles
3	(16-ounce) cans whole tomatoes, crushed
3	bay leaves
1	tablespoon salt
1	tablespoon dried oregano leaves
1	tablespoon red wine vinegar
1	tablespoon brown sugar
3	(16-ounce) cans pinto beans
1	head iceberg lettuce, shredded
1	pound coarsely grated sharp Cheddar cheese
1	bag tortilla chips, lightly crushed

- Brown the ground beef and pork with the onions and garlic in a large heavy pot. Drain off fat and stir in flour and chili powder. Add green chiles, tomatoes, bay leaves, salt, oregano, vinegar and brown sugar. Cover and cook slowly for 2 hours.

- Add beans and cook, uncovered, for 30 minutes more. Put shredded lettuce, grated cheese and crushed chips in serving bowls and let each guest add these to their bowl of chili.

YIELD: 12 SERVINGS

Corn Chowder

6	tablespoons butter or margarine
3/4	cup chopped onions
3/4	cup chopped celery
1/2	cup all-purpose flour
3	cups half-and-half
2	(16-ounce) cans whole kernel corn with juice
2	(16-ounce) cans creamed corn
1/2	teaspoon black pepper
1	teaspoon sugar
3	cups milk
1/2	teaspoon seasoned salt
3	cups chicken stock or canned broth

▸ Melt butter in skillet and sauté onions and celery for about 5 minutes or until soft.

▸ Add flour and cook for 3 minutes, stirring constantly. Add half-and-half and bring to a full boil to thicken while stirring.

▸ Add vegetables and all remaining ingredients to skillet and heat to boiling. Stir to prevent scorching.

YIELD: 12 SERVINGS

Cream of Day Lily Soup

—◦✱◦—

At the same time I'm writing this book, I am also preparing for a progam on Edible Landscaping which I will present at the first annual meeting of CBA — the Cooking and Baking Association of the Professional Association of Innkeepers, in Massachusetts this fall. I came across this recipe and thought it would fit in perfectly with my program. I tested it on some friends without telling them what was in it — they pronounced it delicious. The day lilies have a kind of nutty flavor suggestive of walnuts with a hint of asparagus while the color is a lovely gold similar to pumpkin.

2	cups organically grown yellow or orange day lily buds (use fat buds which are just before opening, not wilted ones)
2	tablespoons olive oil
2	medium shallots, coarsely chopped
2	cloves of garlic, minced
2	cups chicken stock or canned broth
	Zest from 1 lemon
2	tablespoons unsalted butter
2	tablespoons all-purpose flour
1	teaspoon minced fresh thyme
½	teaspoon Tabasco sauce
1	cup half-and-half
	Salt to taste

- Break off stems from day lily buds. Wash well and coarsely chop them.
- Heat olive oil in a medium-sized saucepan. Add shallots and garlic. Cook, stirring often, over medium-low heat for about 5 minutes or until softened but not browned. Add the day lilies and chicken stock. Bring to a boil. Reduce heat and simmer, covered, for about 5 minutes or until day lilies are tender. Remove from heat and strain mixture, separating the liquid from the day lily-shallot mixture.

➳ Cut the zest from the lemon in strips with a vegetable peeler being careful not to get any of the white part of the peel. (Scrape away any of the white part with the tip of a sharp knife.) Purée the strips of lemon peel and day lily-shallot mixture in a blender or food processor, adding just enough of the strained liquid to make a smooth purée. Set aside.

➳ Melt the butter in a large saucepan. Stir in the flour and add the remaining cooking liquid. Cook and stir until thickened and bubbly. Stir in the puréed day lily mixture, thyme and Tabasco sauce and half-and-half. Taste and adjust seasonings, adding salt if needed. Serve warm.

➳ If you wish, purée only half of the day lily mixture and leave the rest chunky. Stir it in with the half-and-half just before serving to add some texture to the soup.

YIELD: 32 SERVINGS

Gazpacho or Gazpacho Mold

3/4	cup 1/8-inch dice green pepper
3/4	cup 1/8-inch dice celery
3/4	cup chopped cucumber
1/3	cup chopped onion
1	(46-ounce) can V-8 vegetable juice
1/4	cup olive oil
1/3	cup red wine vinegar
2	tablespoons Worcestershire sauce
1 1/2	teaspoons salt
1/2	teaspoon pepper
1/2	teaspoon Tabasco sauce
1	teaspoon (1 clove) chopped garlic
3	tablespoons sugar
3	envelopes unflavored gelatin (for mold only)
1	cup sour cream
1	tablespoon or more horseradish to taste

❧ Combine first 13 ingredients in a bowl. Chill overnight. Taste and adjust seasonings before serving. Garnish with sour cream or crème fraîche.

❧ For mold: Make soup as directed above. Dissolve gelatin in a small amount of liquid. Combine with soup; divide into molds and chill overnight. Serve with sour cream-horseradish sauce.

❧ For sauce: Combine sour cream and horseradish; chill.

YIELD: 15 SERVINGS

Crema de Salsa Soup

———— ⟨⟨⟨⟩⟩⟩ ————

3	tablespoons butter
1	large (about 2 cups) onion, chopped
2	cloves of garlic, minced
1	teaspoon ground cumin
	Pinch of white pepper
1½	cups medium-hot picante sauce
1	quart half-and-half
	Grated Cheddar cheese garnish

❧ Melt the butter in a medium skillet over medium heat. Add onion and garlic; cook for about 10 minutes or until soft, stirring occasionally. Stir in cumin and pepper; set aside.

❧ Heat the picante sauce in a 3-quart saucepan over medium heat. Do not boil. Add the onion mixture. Slowly stir in half-and-half and heat through; do not boil. Garnish with Cheddar cheese.

YIELD: 6 SERVINGS

Minted Sweet Pea and Spinach Soup

1/3	cup butter
2	cups finely chopped yellow onions
1	pound frozen chopped spinach, thawed
1	quart chicken broth
1	pound frozen green peas
1½	cups fresh mint leaves
1	cup heavy cream
	Salt and pepper

❧ Melt the butter in a large Dutch oven. Add the onions. Cook, covered, for 25 minutes or until tender and light colored.

❧ Drain the spinach; squeeze out excess liquid. Pour broth into a pot. Stir in the peas and spinach; bring to a boil. Reduce the heat. Simmer, partially covered, for about 20 minutes or until peas are tender.

❧ Pull mint leaves from stems. Rinse and pat dry. When peas are tender, add mint and simmer for 5 minutes.

❧ Pour soup through a strainer, reserving liquid. Process solids in food processor, add some stock and process until smooth.

❧ Return to pot. Add cream and some cooking liquid until of desired consistency.

❧ Season to taste with salt and pepper. Heat briefly to serving temperature.

YIELD: 10 SERVINGS

Potato, Spinach and Leek Soup

———— ⌾⌾⌾ ————

4	cups diced baking potatoes
4	cups sliced leeks (white part and bit of tender green)
6	cups water
1½	teaspoons (or to taste) salt
4	cups fresh spinach
⅔	cup sour cream, heavy cream or crème fraîche (⅓ cup sour cream and ⅓ cup heavy cream whisked together)

❧ Bring potatoes, leeks and water to boil in a 3-quart saucepan. Salt lightly, cover partially and simmer for 20 minutes.

❧ Add the fresh spinach to simmering mixture. Simmer for 5 minutes or until spinach is cooked.

❧ Cool the soup; purée the soup in a blender. Whisk in sour cream, heavy cream or crème fraîche (whichever you prefer).

YIELD: 6 TO 8 SERVINGS OR ABOUT 2½ QUARTS

Okra and Tomato Soup

¼	cup olive oil
½	teaspoon mixed dried oregano, thyme and basil
½	teaspoon red pepper flakes
1	bay leaf
1	cup chopped onion
6	cups V-8 vegetable juice
1½	cups canned tomatoes, undrained, lightly crushed
2	cups water
3	cups sliced fresh or frozen okra

➤ In large soup pot, warm olive oil over very low heat; turn off heat and add dried herbs, red pepper flakes and bay leaf. Stir and let sit for 15 minutes to flavor oil.

➤ Add onion and simmer on lowest heat for 30 minutes or until onion is very soft. Add remaining ingredients and heat.

YIELD: 12 SERVINGS

Tomato, Lemon and Carrot Soup

¼	cup peanut oil
¼	cup butter
3	medium onions, chopped
1½	pounds carrots, peeled, chopped
1	(28-ounce) can whole tomatoes
1	tablespoon lemon rind, pared with potato peeler
1½	quarts chicken stock or canned broth
¾	cup fresh lemon juice

> Heat oil and butter in saucepan. Sauté onions for 5 minutes; add carrots and cook for 2 minutes. Add tomatoes, lemon rind and stock. Bring to a boil and cover pan. Simmer for 30 minutes or until carrots are tender.

> Cool soup and liquefy in blender. Stir in lemon juice.

YIELD: 12 SERVINGS OR ABOUT 3 QUARTS

Red Bell Pepper and Tomato Soup*

3	*large mild white onions, thinly sliced*
2	*tablespoons olive oil*
6	*large red bell peppers, thinly sliced*
6	*large cloves of garlic, peeled*
2	*large carrots, sliced*
1/2	*teaspoon dried thyme leaves*
1/2	*teaspoon dried oregano*
1	*large bay leaf*
1	*(2-inch) strip of orange peel*
	Salt and cayenne pepper to taste
6	*cups chopped canned tomatoes*
5	*cups chicken broth or stock*
1	*tablespoon red wine vinegar*
3	*tablespoons dry sherry*
1	*cup (or more) buttermilk*

> In a large heavy pot, cook onions slowly in oil until soft but not browned. Add peppers, garlic, carrots, herbs and seasonings and cook for 10 more minutes.

> Add tomatoes, broth, vinegar and sherry and simmer for about 30 minutes. Remove from heat and cool. Remove bay leaf and orange peel.

> Blend soup in small batches in blender until smooth. Strain through medium strainer to remove tough particles.

> Just before serving return to heat. Add desired amount of buttermilk, adjust seasoning to taste and serve warm.

YIELD: 12 SERVINGS

Brunswick Stew

Brunswick Stew is traditionally served with barbecue in Georgia. This is a very meaty version which bears no resemblance to the watery, tasteless stuff you get in many barbecue restaurants. It's a lot of trouble to make, but well worth the effort and it freezes well. You can also double or triple the quantity.

6	pounds whole chicken, cooked
3	pounds lean pork loin roast, cooked
3	pounds beef shoulder or chuck roast, cooked
2	(28-ounce) cans whole tomatoes
1	(14-ounce) bottle catsup
1	cup Worcestershire sauce
2	lemons, very thinly sliced, seeds removed
1	cup chopped yellow onion
1/4	pound butter or margarine
1	teaspoon (or more) Tabasco sauce
1	tablespoon each salt and sugar
1/2	teaspoon (or more) black pepper
3	(16-ounce) cans cream-style corn

❧ Cool and shred meat by hand, discarding any gristle but keeping the fat.

❧ Put all the meat in a large heavy pot. I use a cast-iron kettle. Add tomatoes, catsup, Worcestershire sauce, lemons, onion, butter, Tabasco sauce, salt, sugar and pepper and stir well to combine. Cook very slowly for 2 to 3 hours, stirring often to make sure mixture doesn't stick to the bottom of the pot. If it does start to stick badly you'll have to transfer it to another pot or empty and wash the pot it's cooking in. I have found that the creamed corn causes the stew to stick, so I don't add the corn until the last 30 minutes or so of cooking time.

❧ After adding the corn, taste and adjust the seasonings to your preference. The amount of seasonings I have given are approximate. You may want to use less salt or add more catsup, Worcestershire sauce, Tabasco sauce, etc.

❧ When the stew is done, serve immediately or cool it and pack into containers and freeze. Serve with any barbecue, coleslaw, pickles and chips.

YIELD: 18 SERVINGS

Salads and Dressings

Bibb Lettuce Salad with Cranberry Vinaigrette*

This is a wonderful low-calorie summer salad. The fennel is not essential if you can't find any, but if you've never eaten raw fennel, give it a try. You'll be surprised how good it is on a salad like this one.

¼	cup dried cranberries
¼	cup dry red wine
1	shallot, coarsely chopped
2	cups cranberry-raspberry juice
2	tablespoons olive oil
1	tablespoon balsamic vinegar
1	tablespoon minced fresh dill or fennel fronds
2	heads Bibb lettuce
1	small red onion, thinly sliced and separated
1	small fennel bulb, thinly sliced
½	cup dried cranberries

> Place ¼ cup cranberries, wine, shallot and cranberry-raspberry juice in a small nonreactive saucepan. Bring to a boil. Cook over medium heat until you have reduced the liquid to about 1½ cups. Cool.

> Place in a blender and blend until smooth. Measure the oil into a small bowl. Whisk in the cranberry mixture, balsamic vinegar and dill or fennel. Refrigerate.

> Wash lettuce; dry leaves thoroughly. Place in a large bowl. Add the cranberry vinaigrette a small amount at a time. Toss the lettuce with the vinaigrette until the leaves are just barely coated; you may not need all the vinaigrette.

> Arrange the lettuce on 6 salad plates. Garnish with onion, fennel slices and ½ cup cranberries.

YIELD: 6 SERVINGS

Black Bean Salad with Cilantro

2	*pounds dried black beans*
3	*jalapeños, seeded, minced*
2	*red onions, coarsely chopped*
1½	*tablespoons salt*
1	*bunch fresh cilantro, chopped*
1	*tablespoon black pepper*
1	*tablespoon ground cumin*
2	*cloves of garlic, minced*
½	*cup red wine vinegar*
1	*cup olive oil*

- Soak beans in water overnight; drain.
- Boil beans in fresh water for 35 to 40 minutes or until al dente. Drain and cool.
- Combine beans, jalapeños, onions, salt, cilantro and pepper in a bowl. Mix well.
- Mix the remaining ingredients to make the dressing. Pour dressing over bean mixture; toss gently to mix. Chill before serving. Great with fajitas.

YIELD: 10 SERVINGS

Fennel

Kidney Bean Salad*

———∞∞∞———

2	(16-ounce) cans kidney beans
3/4	teaspoon garlic powder
1	dash powdered ginger
1/2	teaspoon dried oregano
2	tablespoons chopped green onions
1/4	teaspoon Tabasco sauce
1/4	cup fresh lemon juice
4	ounces seedless raspberry jelly
3	tablespoons red wine vinegar
	Salt to taste
2	tablespoons olive oil

❧ Combine kidney beans, garlic powder, ginger, oregano, green onions, Tabasco sauce, lemon juice, raspberry jelly, vinegar, salt and olive oil in a bowl and mix well.

❧ Chill until serving time.

YIELD: 6 SERVINGS

Black-Eyed Pea and Corn Salad

½	pound fresh black-eyed peas, or 1 (10-ounce) package frozen
1½	cups fresh or frozen corn kernels
⅓	cup balsamic vinegar
1	tablespoon Dijon mustard
2	tablespoons finely chopped cilantro
2	tablespoons finely chopped parsley
¼	teaspoon dried red pepper flakes
¼	cup extra-virgin olive oil
½	teaspoon salt
1	cup chopped red bell pepper
1	cup (1 medium) chopped red or Vidalia onion
1	cup (2 stalks) chopped celery

❧ Cook the peas in a small amount of lightly salted boiling water in a saucepan for about 20 minutes or until barely tender.

❧ If using fresh corn, cook the same way but only for about 5 minutes. If using frozen corn, just thaw under running water.

❧ Combine the vinegar, mustard, cilantro, parsley, pepper, olive oil and salt in a bowl and mix well.

❧ One hour before serving, combine the peas and corn with other vegetables in a bowl. Add the dressing and toss to mix. Taste and correct seasonings.

YIELD: 6 SERVINGS

No-Egg Caesar Salad

4	anchovies, rinsed, drained
2	large cloves of fresh garlic, peeled
½	cup grated Parmesan cheese
1½	cups mayonnaise
¼	cup red wine vinegar
¼	cup fresh lemon juice
½	cup Dijon mustard
½	teaspoon fresh ground black pepper
2	teaspoons Worcestershire sauce
½	cup vegetable oil
2	tablespoons extra-virgin olive oil
	Romaine lettuce
	Croutons
	Parmesan cheese

🐍 Combine the first 9 ingredients in a blender container. Process until blended. Add the oil in a fine stream, processing constantly until smooth. Keeps several weeks in the refrigerator.

🐍 Wash Romaine lettuce, discarding limp outer leaves. Cut head in half lengthwise and then cut crosswise 3 to 4 times. Refrigerate until serving time.

🐍 Toss lettuce in a covered container with croutons and about 1½ ounces dressing per handful of lettuce. Place on plate and top with freshly grated Parmesan cheese.

YIELD: 12 SERVINGS

Coleslaw with Dill Mayonnaise

———◦◦◦———

1	pound cabbage, red and green
1	medium carrot, grated
½	small red onion, finely chopped
2	tablespoons chopped fresh dill
1	teaspoon lemon juice
¼	teaspoon black pepper
⅔	cup mayonnaise
1½	tablespoons chopped fresh dill
½	teaspoon dry mustard
¼	teaspoon salt
¼	teaspoon paprika
1	shake Tabasco sauce
1	teaspoon horseradish

❧ Core and slice the cabbage in a food processor. Combine the cabbage, carrot, onion, dill, lemon juice and pepper in a bowl and toss to mix.

❧ Combine the remaining ingredients for the dressing. Mix well with the vegetables. Chill.

YIELD: 8 SERVINGS

Cucumbers and Onion*

I rediscovered this classic cucumber dish in a James Beard cookbook, and have updated it a little. My mother used to serve cucumbers this way and we've used it several times for buffets. It would also go well as an accompaniment to a simple summer supper of fresh vegetables and/or grilled meat. You can also use white wine or cider vinegar and fresh dill instead of lime juice and cilantro.

2	cucumbers, peeled
1	medium Vidalia onion
1	teaspoon kosher or regular salt
1	teaspoon freshly ground black pepper
¼	cup fresh lime juice
1	tablespoon chopped fresh cilantro

❧ Cut the cucumbers into halves and scrape out the seeds with a spoon. Cut into thin slices which will look like half-moons.

❧ Halve the onion and slice thin. Sprinkle salt and pepper over onion and cucumbers and let them drain in a colander for 30 minutes.

❧ Rinse the salt off or leave it on as you wish and toss with the lime juice and chopped cilantro.

❧ Chill for an hour or more, draining juices off before serving. Serve cold.

YIELD: 4 SERVINGS

Dublin Potato Salad

This recipe is an interesting combination of potato salad and coleslaw.

2	tablespoons cider vinegar
1	teaspoon celery seeds
1	teaspoon mustard seeds
3	pounds white or red boiling potatoes
2	teaspoons sugar
1/2	teaspoon salt
2	cups shredded cabbage
1/4	cup chopped dill pickle
1/4	cup chopped green onions
1	cup mayonnaise
1/4	cup milk

- Combine the vinegar, celery seeds and mustard seeds in a bowl; set aside.
- Peel and cook potatoes until barely done; don't overcook them. Drain the potatoes. Let them sit until they are cool enough to handle. Cut them into cubes, drizzle with vinegar mixture and sprinkle with sugar and salt, tossing gently to combine seasonings with potatoes.
- Combine shredded cabbage, pickle and green onions in a bowl.
- Mix the mayonnaise and milk together and toss with the cabbage. Gently toss the potatoes and cabbage together. Chill until ready to serve.

YIELD: 10 SERVINGS

Red Potato Salad

2½   *pounds red potatoes, unpeeled,*
       cut into ¼-inch slices
½   *teaspoon salt*
1   *cup mayonnaise*
⅓   *cup sour cream*
½   *teaspoon black pepper*
1½   *tablespoons wine vinegar*
2   *tablespoons finely chopped chives*

- Cook the potatoes in water to cover in a saucepan until barely done; drain well.
- Add the salt, mayonnaise, sour cream, pepper, vinegar and chives and toss to mix. Chill in the refrigerator.

YIELD: 1 SERVING

Chives

Chicken Salad

—◦◦◦—

This chicken salad was our most popular item when we were open for lunch. We rarely make it any more, but I still think it's tasty. This is an exception to my rule about dried herbs. They work fine in this recipe, but the fresh ones would be even better; just double the amount of herbs if using fresh ones.

2	pounds boneless chicken breasts
	Celery leaves
1/2	onion
	Peppercorns
1/2	cup white wine
1	cup chopped celery
1	tablespoon dried parsley flakes
1	teaspoon dried basil leaves
1	teaspoon dried oregano leaves
1/2	teaspoon salt
1/2	teaspoon black pepper
3/4	cup mayonnaise
3/4	cup sour cream

❧ Combine the chicken with enough water to cover in a large shallow saucepan.

❧ Add some celery leaves, half of an onion, a few peppercorns and white wine if you wish. Bring water to a simmer. Lower the heat and gently poach the chicken for 5 or more minutes or just until no longer pink in the center. Do not overcook chicken or it will be tough—this is very important. Cool the chicken and cut into ½-inch cubes. Place the chicken in a large bowl.

❧ Add the celery, herbs and seasonings. Toss to coat the chicken. Add the mayonnaise and sour cream and toss gently. Keep chilled until ready to serve.

YIELD: 8 SERVINGS

Grilled Duckling and Pear Salad

This salad was served for lunch at a culinary professionals meeting which Sandy and I attended in Philadelphia last year. The lunch was sponsored by the Duck Council. We liked the salad so much we came home and recreated it. It's very low in fat and calories, and delicious.

1	recipe Duck Marinade (page 114)
4	boneless duckling breasts, skin removed
2	recipes Honey Dijon Vinaigrette (page 66)
4	firm ripe pears
8	cups mixed salad greens
½	cup chopped walnuts, toasted
4	ounces Gorgonzola cheese, crumbled

➤ Marinate duck breasts overnight. Make a double recipe of Honey Dijon Vinaigrette.

➤ Dry breasts with paper towels. Preheat broiler or grill. Broil or grill each side of duck breast on medium-high heat for about 4 minutes, turn and grill each side for 2 more minutes; breasts should be cooked to medium doneness, still a little pink in the center. Set aside to cool.

➤ Peel and core pears, and slice into crescent-shaped wedges. Lay pear slices on a baking pan that has been lightly sprayed with nonstick cooking spray, then lightly spray pears also. Bake pears in oven at 425 degrees for about 7 minutes on each side or until golden brown.

➤ Toss salad greens with half of the vinaigrette and divide evenly among dinner plates. Arrange pear wedges around edge of each salad. Slice each duck breast on the diagonal into 6 slices. Arrange 3 slices of duck in center of each salad. Sprinkle with walnuts and crumbled cheese. Pass additional vinaigrette at the table.

YIELD: 8 SERVINGS

Tuna Salad

1½   pounds fresh tuna
2   celery stalks, roughly chopped
2   cups chopped celery
4   hard-boiled eggs
¾   cup dill pickles, chopped
1   cup mayonnaise
½   cup sour cream
2   tablespoons capers
1   teaspoon seasoned salt

- Simmer tuna in water with celery in a large skillet for 10 minutes or until just barely done.
- Mix with the chopped celery, eggs, pickles, mayonnaise, sour cream, capers and seasoned salt in a large bowl.
- Serve over lettuce or as a sandwich spread.

YIELD: 6 SERVINGS

Rosemary

Pasta Salad with
Wild Mushrooms and Olives*

This is a nice dish for a buffet; we have used it for several wedding buffets this spring. If you use the kind of sun-dried tomatoes that are packed in oil, don't soak them, just rinse and use as is. You can leave out the dried mushrooms if you don't have any, but they do add wonderful flavor. You can also substitute other kinds of fresh mushrooms or just use the cultivated kind found in any supermarket.

6	ounces pitted jumbo ripe olives
1/4	cup red wine vinegar
1/2	cup olive oil
2	cloves of garlic, minced
3	slices bacon
1/2	cup sun-dried tomatoes, cut in julienne strips
1/4	cup white wine
1/4	cup dried morels or mixed wild mushrooms
1	pound rotelle pasta
3/4	cup freshly grated Parmesan cheese
	Salt and pepper to taste
6	ounces shiitake mushrooms
3/4	pound button mushrooms
3	tablespoons butter or olive oil
3	tablespoons freshly chopped parsley
3	tablespoons chopped fresh basil or other mild herbs

- ➤ At least 6 hours ahead, drain olives, cut into quarters and marinate with wine vinegar, olive oil and minced garlic.
- ➤ Cook bacon until crisp and drain, reserving bacon grease. Crumble bacon and set aside.

- In a small bowl, soak sun-dried tomato strips with white wine and just enough water to cover tomatoes for 30 minutes or until softened.

- In another small bowl, soak the dried mushrooms in just enough water to cover until softened.

- Cook the pasta in a large pot of boiling salted water until just barely tender — al dente. Drain and rinse briefly with cold running water; drain well and while still warm, toss with reserved bacon grease, half of the grated Parmesan cheese and salt and pepper to taste.

- Slice the shiitake and button mushrooms and lightly sauté in butter or oil for 1 to 2 minutes. Set aside.

- Drain and squeeze soaking liquid from sun-dried tomatoes and dried mushrooms, reserving liquid. Chop mushrooms if needed so they are all about the same size.

- One hour before serving, drain the olives, reserving marinade.

- Add the olives to the pasta with chopped bacon, dried tomatoes and mushrooms, and sautéed mushrooms, adding some of the oil marinade and some of the reserved soaking juices for flavor. Taste and adjust seasonings.

- Sprinkle with remaining Parmesan cheese, parsley and basil. Serve at room temperature.

YIELD: 8 SERVINGS

Bleu Cheese Dressing

This recipe appeared in my first book also, but it's so good that I felt it deserved to be in this one too. It's great as a dip for raw vegetables or on a traditional American tossed salad. It's a fairly heavy dressing, though, so use sturdy greens such as iceberg or romaine lettuce that won't wilt under the weight of the dressing.

1	cup mayonnaise
3/4	cup sour cream
1/4	teaspoon granulated garlic
1/4	teaspoon granulated onion
1/8	teaspoon salt
1/4	teaspoon pepper
1 1/2	teaspoons dried parsley flakes
1/2	cup milk
1 1/2	cups crumbled bleu cheese

Whisk all ingredients except bleu cheese together in a bowl. Stir in bleu cheese. Chill well before serving. Will keep at least a week.

YIELD: 1 QUART

Honey Dijon Vinaigrette*

2	tablespoons Dijon mustard
2	tablespoons white wine vinegar
2	tablespoons honey
3	tablespoons olive oil

In bowl, blend mustard, vinegar, honey and oil. Store in refrigerator. Will keep up to 2 weeks.

YIELD: 6 SERVINGS

Herb Vinaigrette

½	cup white wine vinegar
¼	cup Dijon mustard
1	teaspoon salt
1	teaspoon black pepper
1	cup olive oil
1	cup peanut, vegetable or light olive oil
½	cup fresh basil leaves, stems removed

❧ In blender, purée vinegar, mustard, salt and pepper. Add oil slowly. Add basil leaves and blend briefly just until basil is finely chopped but still distinctly visible.

❧ Will keep at least a week in the refrigerator, but flavor is best when fresh.

YIELD: 6 SERVINGS OR 1 PINT

Lemon Dill Vinaigrette

1	cup fresh lemon juice
1½	teaspoons salt
¼	teaspoon pepper
1	tablespoon honey
2	tablespoons roughly chopped onion
3	cups oil
¼	cup fresh dill, no stems

❧ Purée lemon juice, salt, pepper, honey and onion in blender.

❧ Add oil slowly.

❧ Add dill and blend briefly.

YIELD: 12 SERVINGS OR 1 QUART

Lime Honey Yogurt Fruit Sauce

2	*large limes, grated rind and juice*
1	*pint plain nonfat yogurt*
¾	*cup honey*
2	*tablespoons chopped fresh mint*

- Grate zest from limes and squeeze juice. Combine with yogurt, honey and mint.
- Toss with cut melons and other mixed fruit.

YIELD: 8 SERVINGS

Mint

Pepper Parmesan Salad Dressing

———ᘓᘈᘊᘈᘊᘈ———

2	cups mayonnaise
2	tablespoons lemon juice
1	teaspoon cider vinegar
3/4	teaspoon garlic, granulated
1 1/2	teaspoons black pepper, coarse
1/2	teaspoon salt
1 1/2	teaspoons Worcestershire sauce
1	shake Tabasco sauce
1/4	cup Parmesan cheese
1	cup buttermilk

❧ Whisk mayonnaise, lemon juice, vinegar, garlic, pepper, salt, Worcestershire sauce and Tabasco sauce together, adding Parmesan cheese and buttermilk last.

❧ Will keep several weeks in refrigerator.

YIELD: 12 SERVINGS OR 1 QUART

Poppy Seed Dressing

Serve this with Spinach and Strawberry Salad or any fruit salad.

2	tablespoons coarsely chopped onion
1/3	cup honey
1/2	teaspoon salt
	Dash white pepper
1/3	cup white wine or cider vinegar
2 1/2	tablespoons Dijon mustard
1/2	teaspoon powdered ginger
1	shake Tabasco sauce
1	cup salad oil
1 1/3	tablespoons poppy seeds

Combine onion, honey, salt, pepper, vinegar, mustard, ginger and Tabasco sauce in blender. Slowly add oil. Remove from blender and stir in poppy seeds.

YIELD: 4 SERVINGS OR ABOUT 2 CUPS

Breads

New Age Beaten Biscuits with Country Ham

I remember beaten biscuits from my childhood. I'm not sure who in our family had the patience to do the amount of beating required to make them. It was probably a faithful black cook, employed by one of my more affluent aunts, who did the beating. Anyway I remember them and when I came across a recipe for making them in the food processor, I was intrigued. I tried it, and it worked. They may not be as good as those beaten for ages by hand, but I'll bet none of us will have any competition in that department! Try these, they're more like a cracker than a biscuit and I think they're very good. By the way, Craig Claiborne gets the credit for coming up with the modern method. This recipe makes 10 to 12 biscuits. I would not try to double the quantity unless you have a very heavy-duty professional food processor. Just make several batches for a crowd.

2	cups all-purpose flour
1	teaspoon salt
8	tablespoons very cold butter
1/2	cup ice water
1/2	pound unsalted butter, softened
1	tablespoon Dijon mustard
1	tablespoon finely chopped fresh dill
1/2	pound cooked country ham, thinly sliced

❧ Put the flour in the food processor. Add the salt and process briefly to combine.

❧ Cut the very cold butter into tiny pieces and add it all at once to the food processor. Process until the mixture resembles coarse meal. Leave the processor running and add the ice water slowly through the food tube, processing until the mixture forms a ball and continue to process for 2 minutes. You may have to hold your processor on the table for this last step. Mine doesn't act like it really enjoys beating this dough any more than those old cooks did, but it does perform the job.

✌ Transfer the dough onto a lightly floured surface. Roll into a ⅛-inch-thick rectangle; fold it in half to make 2 layers. Cut into rounds of desired size with a biscuit cutter. Usually these are cut smaller than a normal biscuit, about 1½ inches is a good size. Bake at 350 degrees for about 25 to 35 minutes or until golden brown. Split them in half and if they are still soft in the center you can return the halves to the oven briefly to crisp.

✌ Make the dill butter by combining the softened butter, mustard and dill in the food processor. Slice the country ham as thin as possible and cut into small pieces a little larger than the biscuits.

✌ To serve, spread 1 side of biscuits with dill butter, place a small piece of country ham on top and replace the top of the biscuit.

✌ These biscuits will keep for several days in an airtight tin.

YIELD: 10 TO 12 SERVINGS

Dill

Oat Bran Scones

———

1/3	cup All-Bran cereal
1/2	cup buttermilk
2	tablespoons heavy cream
1 3/4	cups all-purpose flour
1 1/2	teaspoons baking powder
1/2	teaspoon baking soda
1/4	cup sugar
6	tablespoons cold unsalted butter, cut into 1/4-inch pieces
1/2	cup heavy cream
3/4	teaspoon sugar

- Preheat convection oven to 325 degrees or conventional oven to 400 degrees.
- In small bowl, stir All-Bran into buttermilk and 2 tablespoons cream and soak to soften All-Bran.
- In large mixing bowl, sift together flour, baking powder, baking soda and 1/4 cup sugar.
- Add butter pieces and mix with hands or pastry blender until mixture resembles coarse crumbs.
- Add buttermilk-bran mixture and stir just until mixture forms a dough. Add 1 tablespoon more buttermilk if mixture is too dry to hold together.
- Turn dough out onto a well-floured surface and shape into a ball, flatten ball to a circle about 1/2 inch thick and cut with a 2-inch biscuit cutter to make 16 round scones. Or, to make traditional wedge-shape scones divide dough into 2 equal balls, roll each into a circle 1/2 inch thick and cut into 8 equal wedges.
- Brush tops of scones with 1/2 cup cream and sprinkle with 3/4 teaspoon sugar.
- Bake for 15 to 20 minutes or until browned and crisp. Note: If freezing scones for later use, bake for only 10 minutes or until they are done but just barely beginning to brown, remove, cool and freeze. Thaw and heat at 325 degrees for 5 to 10 minutes before serving.

YIELD: 16 SERVINGS

Lemon Poppy Seed Muffins*

1¼   cups flour
¾   cup whole wheat flour
½   cup sugar
2   tablespoons poppy seeds
2   teaspoons baking powder
1   teaspoon baking soda
½   teaspoon salt
2   teaspoons grated lemon rind
1   egg
¾   cup nonfat yogurt
¼   cup lemon juice
3   tablespoons skim milk
1   tablespoon butter, melted

- Preheat oven to 400 degrees. Spray muffin tins with nonstick cooking spray.
- Combine the dry ingredients in a large bowl. In separate bowl, blend liquid ingredients. Stir liquid ingredients into dry ingredients just until moistened. Batter will be thick—don't overbeat. Pour batter into muffin tins.
- Bake at 400 degrees for 18 to 22 minutes or until muffins test done.

YIELD: 12 SERVINGS

Apple Butter Muffins

½	pound unsalted butter, softened
1½	cups sugar
4½	cups all-purpose flour
2½	tablespoons baking powder
¾	teaspoon salt
1½	teaspoons nutmeg
3	eggs
1½	cups milk
¾	cup apple butter
¾	pound butter, melted
1	tablespoon cinnamon
1½	cups sugar

- Preheat oven to 350 degrees.
- In mixer on medium speed, cream butter and sugar until fluffy.
- In a separate bowl, sift flour, baking powder, salt and nutmeg together.
- Combine eggs with butter and sugar in mixer, then add flour mixture alternately with milk, mixing well until blended.
- Line muffin tins with paper liners.
- Divide batter in half and distribute ½ of the mixture evenly into muffin cups. Make depression in batter in each cup and fill with a generous teaspoon of apple butter. Divide second half of batter among cups, spreading to cover apple butter.
- Bake at 350 degrees for 20 to 25 minutes or until golden brown.
- Let cool for 5 minutes. Dip tops of muffins in melted butter, then in cinnamon-sugar mixture. These muffins freeze very well.

YIELD: 36 MUFFINS

Corn Muffins

These have been a staple in our bread baskets since we opened. A few years ago we added sour cream to the recipe which was a good improvement. They will keep, wrapped with foil, in the refrigerator for a couple of days or they can be frozen and reheated.

$1^3/4$ *cups 3 Rivers Brand self-rising*
                   cornmeal mix
$3/4$ *cup milk*
1   *cup canned cream corn*
1   *egg*
$1/4$ *cup sour cream*
                  Cracked black pepper to taste

- Grease muffin tins well. Place mix in large bowl.
- Add milk, corn, egg and sour cream. Stir just until combined.
- Scoop mix into muffin tins, filling ⅔ full.
- Sprinkle tops of batter with cracked pepper.
- Bake at 375 degrees for 30 minutes or until tops spring back and are nicely browned.

YIELD: 8 MUFFINS

Banana Bread

This is the best banana bread recipe I've seen. It's very moist and freezes beautifully. Every inn has to make banana bread because we always have overripe bananas on hand. Make two loaves and put one in the freezer. Spread some Tangy Cream Cheese Spread (page 80) on each slice for a special treat.

4	ounces butter, softened
2	cups sugar
4	eggs
2	teaspoons vanilla extract
3	cups flour
2	teaspoons baking soda
1/8	teaspoon salt
1	cup sour cream
3	cups mashed bananas
1	cup chopped pecans or walnuts

- Preheat oven to 350 degrees. Grease and flour two 5x9-inch loaf pans.
- Cream butter and sugar in mixer on medium speed. Add eggs and vanilla and beat for 1½ minutes. Combine the flour, baking soda and salt. Add to the creamed mixture alternately with the sour cream.
- Stir in the bananas and nuts. Mix until well blended. Pour into prepared loaf pans. Bake at 350 degrees for 1 hour or until bread tests done.

YIELD: 24 SERVINGS

Date Nut Prune Bread*

½ cup chopped pitted dates
½ cup chopped pitted prunes
1 cup coarsely chopped walnuts
1½ teaspoons baking soda
½ teaspoon salt
3 tablespoons shortening
¾ cup boiling water
2 eggs
¾ cup sugar
1½ cups all-purpose flour

- Preheat oven to 350 degrees.
- Grease a 5x9-inch loaf pan.
- Combine the dates, prunes, walnuts, baking soda, salt and shortening in a bowl. Pour in the boiling water and stir well. Let mixture stand for 15 minutes.
- Beat the eggs and sugar together with a fork. Add the flour and stir. Dough will be too stiff to mix very well, but that's okay.
- Add the date mixture and mix until batter is well blended. Pour into the loaf pan.
- Bake at 350 degrees for 1 hour or until a toothpick inserted in center comes out clean.

YIELD: 12 SERVINGS

Tangy Cream Cheese Spread

8   ounces cream cheese, softened
½   cup good quality orange or other
          tangy fruit marmalade

❧ Combine cream cheese and marmalade in food processor or by hand.

❧ Refrigerate several hours to blend flavors. Will keep a week in the refrigerator.

❧ Serve with Banana Bread (page 78) or Date Nut Prune Bread (page 79).

YIELD: 24 (1-TABLESPOON) SERVINGS

Lemon Balm

Refrigerator Bran Muffins

4	large eggs
2	cups sugar
8	ounces butter, melted
2	cups black coffee
4	cups buttermilk
6	cups All-Bran cereal
5	cups flour
1	tablespoon plus 2 teaspoons baking soda

- Whisk together eggs, sugar and butter.
- Add coffee, buttermilk and cereal to egg mixture.
- Let sit until cereal gets soggy.
- Mix together flour and baking soda. Add to soggy mixture.
- Keeps in refrigerator for 1 week.
- Add 1 cup chopped nuts, raisins or dried cranberries to batter just before baking. Spoon into greased and floured muffin cups.
- Bake at 375 degrees for 20 minutes or until muffins test done.

YIELD: 24 SERVINGS

Zucchini Cheese Bread

Everyone who grows zucchini in the summer needs new ways to use it. This is a lovely savory bread which freezes beautifully and is great toasted for breakfast or with soup or salad for lunch.

4   eggs
½   cup honey
¼   cup unsalted butter, melted
1½ cups sour cream
3   cups grated fresh zucchini, not peeled
4   cups unbleached all-purpose flour
1   teaspoon salt
4   teaspoons baking powder
1   teaspoon baking soda
1   cup grated Parmesan cheese

- Preheat oven to 350 degrees. Grease two 5x9-inch loaf pans.
- Beat eggs in a large bowl until light and slightly thick. Beat in honey, melted butter and sour cream. Stir in zucchini and mix well.
- Sift flour, salt, baking powder and baking soda together in a separate bowl. Sprinkle cheese over the flour mixture and toss with a fork, distributing cheese evenly.
- Add the flour mixture to the zucchini mixture. Fold gently just to combine. DO NOT OVERMIX!
- Pour into the prepared loaf pans. Bake at 350 degrees for 45 to 55 minutes or until the top feels springy. Let cool for 10 minutes and remove from pans.

YIELD: 12 SERVINGS

Breakfast and Brunch

After Easter Eggs

We would serve this with North Georgia Stone Ground Grits from Logan Turnpike Mill in Blairsville, Georgia, which we sell at the inn. They can also be ordered directly—call 706-745-5735.

4	*hard-boiled eggs*
1	*cup chopped cooked bacon or ham (optional)*
2	*cups Mornay Sauce (page 85)*
1	*cup coarse fresh bread crumbs*
1/4	*cup melted butter*

> Peel and slice eggs. Place in 1 layer in bottom of buttered shallow baking dish or 4 small individual ovenproof dishes.

> Sprinkle bacon or ham on top of eggs. Spread warm Mornay Sauce over eggs.

> Combine bread crumbs with melted butter and sprinkle over sauce.

> Bake at 400 degrees for 5 minutes or until crumbs have browned and casserole is heated through.

> Serve immediately with North Georgia Stone Ground Grits and fruit.

YIELD: 4 SERVINGS

Eggs Mornay

—◦◦◦—

4   *eggs*
4   *pieces Canadian bacon*
4   *English muffin halves, buttered,*
       lightly toasted
       Mornay Sauce

❧ Poach eggs and hold in bowl of very hot water until just before serving.

❧ Warm Canadian bacon briefly in pan on stove or in oven just before serving. Place warm toasted English muffins on serving plates. Place 1 piece bacon on top of each English muffin half, top with poached eggs and spoon warm Mornay Sauce over eggs. Garnish with chopped parsley or paprika if desired. Serve immediately.

YIELD: 4 SERVINGS

Mornay Sauce

½   *cup unsalted butter*
½   *cup all-purpose flour*
2   *cups milk*
¼   *teaspoon cayenne pepper*
1   *teaspoon Worcestershire sauce*
    Salt to taste
2   *cups sharp shredded Cheddar cheese or*
      use part other cheeses such as
      Parmesan, Swiss, etc.

❧ This can be done the day before and reheated slowly in a saucepan or in a microwave. Melt butter in a medium saucepan. Stir in flour and cook over medium heat for 1 minute, stirring constantly. Do not brown. Remove pan from heat and whisk in milk.

❧ Return pan to heat and cook until mixture thickens, whisking constantly. Add cayenne, Worcestershire sauce and salt. Stir in cheeses and continue stirring until mixture is smooth. Taste and correct seasonings. Keep warm or refrigerate until needed and reheat.

Scrambled Egg Casserole

This has been one of our favorite Saturday morning breakfast dishes for several years. We love its versatility. You can prepare the ingredients ahead and throw it together that morning which is what we usually do, or you can do the whole thing ahead and reheat it just before serving. To prepare ahead, bake casserole until eggs are just barely set, about 10 minutes, then refrigerate or wrap tightly and freeze. To reheat, thaw in refrigerator 1 day if frozen, cover top with aluminum foil and heat at 325 degrees for about 20 minutes or until thoroughly warmed, turn up heat and brown crumbs.

2	tablespoons butter
1/2	cup chopped cooked ham
1/4	cup chopped green onions
1/2	cup sliced mushrooms
1/2	cup chopped Roma tomatoes
1/2	(10-ounce) package frozen chopped spinach, thawed, drained
2	tablespoons butter
2 1/2	tablespoons flour
2	cups milk
1/2	teaspoon salt
1/4	teaspoon pepper
1	cup shredded sharp Cheddar cheese
1/4	teaspoon seasoned salt
8	eggs, beaten slightly
2	tablespoons butter
2	cups soft bread crumbs
2	tablespoons melted butter

Melt 2 tablespoons butter in a nonstick skillet. Sauté ham, green onions, mushrooms and tomatoes in the skillet lightly until soft. Stir in the spinach and place vegetables in a colander to drain. Wipe skillet clean.

➢ Melt 2 tablespoons butter in a medium saucepan. Stir in flour. Cook for 2 minutes, stirring with a whisk. Add milk slowly. Bring to a boil. Cook until mixture has thickened, whisking constantly. Turn down heat and add salt, pepper and shredded cheese. Stir until cheese has melted and sauce is smooth. Correct seasonings.

➢ Add seasoned salt to eggs. Melt 2 tablespoons butter in the skillet. Soft scramble the eggs over low heat until about half cooked, stirring often with a wooden spoon. Add 2 cups of cheese sauce to eggs and combine well; remove from heat while eggs are still very soft and runny. (They will finish cooking in the oven.)

➢ Spray bottom of 2-quart casserole with nonstick cooking spray. Layer ½ of the scrambled eggs in bottom of pan, cover with sautéed vegetables and top with the rest of the scrambled eggs.

➢ Mix bread crumbs with 2 tablespoons butter. Cover top of casserole with buttered bread crumbs. Bake at 375 to 400 degrees for 15 minutes or until eggs are set and crumbs are browned.

YIELD: 8 SERVINGS

Scrambled Eggs with Cream Cheese and Basil

I like fresh basil in almost everything, and especially in scrambled eggs.

> 12 large eggs
> ½ teaspoon seasoned salt
> 2 ounces cream cheese, cut into cubes
> 2 tablespoons unsalted butter
> 4 fresh basil leaves, chopped

➢ Break eggs into blender. Add seasoned salt and cream cheese. Blend until cream cheese is thoroughly mixed with eggs.

➢ Melt butter in a large nonstick skillet and add eggs. Cook over low heat until eggs are almost set, stirring constantly once eggs begin to cook.

➢ Stir basil into eggs just before they are completely done. Serve immediately.

YIELD: 6 SERVINGS

Rolled Omelet Soufflé

6	tablespoons butter
$1/2$	cup plus 2 tablespoons flour
$1/2$	teaspoon salt
	Dash of cayenne pepper
$2 1/4$	cups milk
6	eggs, separated
$1/4$	cup chopped green pepper
$1/2$	cup chopped onion
2	tablespoons butter
$1/2$	cup diced seeded tomatoes
$1/2$	cup sliced mushrooms

- Grease a 10½x15½-inch jelly roll pan and line with waxed paper or foil. Grease the paper or foil.

- Make cream sauce by melting 6 tablespoons butter in a large skillet over low heat. Blend in the flour. Cook over low heat for 3 minutes, stirring constantly. Stir in the salt and cayenne pepper. Add the milk gradually, stirring to blend well. Cook until thickened, stirring constantly.

- Beat the egg yolks in a bowl. Stir a small amount of the hot cream sauce into the egg yolks. Add the egg yolks to the cream sauce, mixing well. Set aside to cool.

- Prepare filling—sauté pepper and onion in 2 tablespoons butter until soft. Add tomatoes and mushrooms and cook briefly. Drain in colander to remove excess juices from tomatoes. Set aside where it will stay warm.

- Beat egg whites, fold into cooled sauce and spread into prepared pan. Bake for 15 minutes or more at 375 degrees or until puffed and brown.

- Remove from oven. Invert onto a greased piece of waxed paper or foil which is several inches longer than the pan. Spread with the filling and roll up lengthwise like a jelly roll by lifting the foil underneath and pushing the soufflé into a roll. Place a platter at the end of the paper and make the final roll onto the platter. If the roll tears or looks less than perfect, sprinkle the top with a mixture of buttered toasted bread crumbs, fresh herbs and/or Parmesan cheese.

- Keep warm in a low oven if not serving immediately. I find that the finished omelet will hold just fine in the oven for up to 30 minutes.

YIELD: 8 SERVINGS

Spinach Quiche

—◦/◦/◦—

I know there's nothing new about a spinach quiche, but this is the best quiche recipe I've ever seen. Of course that's because it uses heavy cream. You can use milk or half-and-half, but it won't have the creamy texture you get from cream. This quiche will freeze nicely also.

1	deep-dish pie crust
1	(10-ounce) package frozen spinach, thawed
3	tablespoons butter
3	tablespoons finely chopped green onions
3/4	teaspoon salt
1	dash of pepper
	Pinch of nutmeg
4	eggs
2	cups heavy cream

❧ Prick crust bottom and side. Prebake crust at 350 degrees for 8 to 10 minutes or just until dough is set, but crust has not begun to brown. To keep crust from "bubbling" you can place pie weights or dried beans in bottom of crust which has been lined with a square of foil before baking. Bake for 5 minutes, remove weights and bake a few more minutes or until crust no longer looks raw. Set aside to cool.

❧ Sauté the spinach in 1 tablespoon of butter in a skillet until dry.

❧ Sauté the onions in the remaining 2 tablespoons butter in a small skillet until soft. Add to the spinach. Add the seasonings. Cook until all the liquid is evaporated.

❧ Whisk together eggs and heavy cream in a bowl.

❧ Add the spinach mixture gradually to the egg mixture, combining well. Pour into the cooled pie shell.

❧ Bake at 350 degrees for 25 to 35 minutes or until quiche is firm.

YIELD: 6 SERVINGS

Potato Breakfast Casserole

4	baking potatoes or 2½ pounds red potatoes, cut into 2-inch dice
2	large red or green sweet peppers
1	large onion
	Butter
½	pound smoked sausage, cut into ½-inch dice
8	eggs
¼	pound sharp Cheddar cheese, grated

- Parboil potatoes for 5 to 10 minutes or just until barely tender. Dice peppers and onion into ½-inch pieces.
- Sauté the onion in butter. Add the peppers and cook until tender. Set aside.
- Sauté the sausage and parboiled potatoes in butter over high heat until lightly browned; drain.
- Combine the potatoes, sausage and vegetables in a 9x13-inch baking dish, spreading evenly.
- Make 8 holes in mixture with spoon and break an egg into each hole. Cover evenly with cheese.
- Bake at 350 degrees for about 30 minutes or until eggs are set.
- May substitute zucchini for the sweet peppers or use a combination of the two.

YIELD: 8 SERVINGS

Blintz Casserole

<del>๑/๑/๑</del>

This is a wonderful dish for a brunch—rich and slightly sweet, and a nice change from the usual breakfast casserole. I would serve it with mixed fruit and some good sausages or Canadian bacon. Make it up the night before and pop it in the oven early in the morning. It does take a while to cook.

2	pounds ricotta cheese
2	eggs
1/4	cup sugar
1/8	teaspoon salt
1/4	cup fresh lemon juice
8	ounces cream cheese, softened
1/2	pound butter or margarine, melted
2	eggs
1/2	cup sugar
1	cup sifted flour
1	tablespoon baking powder
1/8	teaspoon salt
1/4	cup milk
1	teaspoon vanilla extract

๑➤ Place the ricotta cheese, eggs, sugar, salt, lemon juice and cream cheese in mixer and blend well for filling. Set aside.

๑➤ Mix the remaining ingredients for the batter by hand.

๑➤ Spoon ½ of the batter into a greased 9x13-inch baking dish. Top with filling, spreading it on top. Spread remaining batter over the filling.

๑➤ Bake at 300 degrees for 1½ hours.

YIELD: 12 SERVINGS

Blueberry Buttermilk Pancakes with Toasted Walnut Butter

These have been a morning tradition here since we opened. On Sunday I usually cook them at the buffet table in the dining room so guests can have them right off the griddle. They really are the best pancakes I have ever eaten. Some people tell me they can't get theirs to taste like mine and I think the secret is the buttermilk baking mix we use which is only available commercially. I'm going to start packaging it for sale to guests. If using frozen blueberries, put them in a colander and thaw briefly under running water, then let them drain for a few minutes. This helps keep them from turning the batter blue.

½	cup Granola (optional) (page 96)
2	eggs
2	cups buttermilk
2	cups Glen-Ella baking mix or a purchased buttermilk baking mix
1	cup fresh or frozen blueberries
1	tablespoon melted butter (optional)
	Toasted Wanut Butter

2➤ Preheat electric griddle to 400 degrees. Have nonstick spray can ready to spray griddle before each batch of pancakes.

2➤ If using granola, blend in a blender to fine crumbs.

2➤ Beat eggs in a mixing bowl. Whisk in buttermilk and granola.

2➤ Gently stir in baking mix and blueberries. Add 1 tablespoon butter if desired. Batter should be thick enough to plop from spoon.

2➤ Ladle 1½ ounces of batter onto griddle for each pancake and cook until bubbles form on surface. Turn over the pancake and cook until done. Serve at once with Toasted Walnut Butter and maple syrup.

YIELD: 6 SERVINGS

Toasted Walnut Butter

8	ounces butter, softened (or 4 ounces each butter and margarine)
½	cup packed light brown sugar
½	teaspoon maple flavoring (optional)
½	cup finely chopped toasted walnuts

Cream 8 ounces butter and brown sugar in a food processor or mixer until well combined. Add flavoring and walnuts. Spoon into a serving bowl and chill until firm. May also be frozen.

Rosemary

Lou's French Toast

4	eggs, beaten slightly
1/4	cup sugar
1/4	teaspoon nutmeg
2/3	cup orange juice
1/3	cup milk
1/2	teaspoon vanilla extract
1	(18-ounce) loaf sourdough or French bread
2/3	cup melted butter
1/2	cup chopped pecans
	Confectioners' sugar

❧ Combine first 6 ingredients in blender or with whisk the day before serving.

❧ Slice bread into slices about ¾ inch thick. Place bread slices close together in a shallow dish. Pour liquid over the bread, coating completely. Refrigerate overnight, turning bread once after about an hour.

❧ Drizzle butter over bottom of a baking sheet with sides. Arrange bread slices on top of butter in pan, sides not touching. Sprinkle pecans on top of bread slices.

❧ Bake at 350 degrees for about 20 minutes or until puffed and golden brown. Sprinkle with confectioners' sugar.

❧ Serve with maple syrup, preserves or Orange Sauce for French Toast (page 95).

YIELD: 6 SERVINGS

Orange Sauce for French Toast

Buy some Bahamian coconut rum if you go to the Bahamas—if you don't have the real thing, leave it out.

2	*navel oranges*
2	*cups orange juice, fresh if possible*
	Juice of 1 fresh lime
1	*small can unsweetened pineapple juice*
1/4	*cup Bahamian coconut rum*
1	*cup dried cranberries (optional)*
1/2	*cup sugar*
1	*tablespoon butter*
2	*tablespoons cornstarch*

- Finely grate zest from 1 of the oranges, being sure to get only the outside orange part of the peel, leaving the bitter white part on the orange.
- Peel oranges with sharp knife, cutting away all the membrane from the outside, then remove each orange section by cutting down the sides of each membrane until the section pops loose.
- Combine orange, lime and pineapple juices with orange zest in a saucepan. Add coconut rum, dried cranberries and sugar.
- Cook over medium heat, stirring to dissolve the sugar. Add butter and cornstarch which has been dissolved in a little water or juice. Bring to a boil. Cook until mixture has thickened somewhat, stirring constantly.
- Cool and set aside. Stir in orange sections just before serving.
- Drizzle over Lou's French Toast (page 94) and pass extra sauce at the table.

YIELD: 8 SERVINGS

Granola

—∞∞∞—

We make this in large quantities and store it in the freezer. I would recommend this to you also because it's too much trouble to make in small amounts. It also makes wonderful gifts for friends.

½	cup margarine
1½	cups honey
7	cups regular oats (not instant)
1	cup sliced almonds
1	cup roasted sunflower seed kernels
1	cup chopped pecans
1	teaspoon ground cinnamon
1	cup raisins
1	cup diced dried apricots

➢ Melt margarine in a small saucepan over low heat. Add the honey. Warm over low heat until honey has thinned. Set aside and keep warm.

➢ Combine oats, almonds, sunflower seed kernels, pecans and cinnamon in a large bowl. Add margarine-honey mixture and stir thoroughly.

➢ Place the mixture in a large shallow pan such as a jelly roll pan or roasting pan in a shallow, even layer. (You may need more than 1 pan.)

➢ Bake at 275 degrees for about 45 minutes or until browned and crisp, stirring mixture every 10 minutes. Remove from oven; add raisins and apricots while still warm.

➢ Let cool, pack into sealable plastic bags or airtight jars and freeze.

YIELD: 12 CUPS

Vegetables

Marinated Asparagus*

2	pounds fresh asparagus
1	large or 2 small navel oranges
5	large fresh sage leaves
2	tablespoons raspberry-flavored wine vinegar
1/4	teaspoon salt
1/2	cup olive oil
1/2	cup pistachio nuts

➤ Make this the day before serving. Cut tough ends from asparagus; if they are large ones, it helps to peel the tough outer skin from the bottom ½ of the stalk with a vegetable peeler. Steam the asparagus in a vegetable steamer for about 4 minutes, or simmer briefly in water in a skillet until just barely tender. Drain and set aside to cool.

➤ With a vegetable peeler, strip five 2-inch strips from oranges, being careful to remove only the orange-colored rind, not any of the bitter white part. If some of the white pith comes off with the strip, scrape it off the peel using the tip of a sharp knife.

➤ Squeeze oranges and place juice in food processor. Add strips of rind, fresh sage, raspberry vinegar and salt. Process until no solids are visible. Add olive oil in a slow stream and blend until dressing is smooth. Add pistachios and blend until they are incorporated into dressing. Pour dressing over asparagus and marinate for 24 hours. Serve cold or at room temperature.

YIELD: 8 SERVINGS

Broccoli Mold

2	(10-ounce) packages frozen chopped broccoli
6	hard-cooked eggs, chopped
1/2	teaspoon seasoned salt
1	envelope unflavored gelatin
1	can beef bouillon or consomme
1	cup mayonnaise
2	tablespoons lemon juice
2	tablespoons Worcestershire sauce
1/4	teaspoon Tabasco sauce
1/4	cup chopped green onions

~ Cook broccoli according to package directions; drain and cool.

~ Combine broccoli with chopped eggs and salt.

~ Soften gelatin in ¼ cup beef bouillon.

~ Heat remaining bouillon to boiling, stir in gelatin until dissolved. Cool and combine with broccoli mixture.

~ Blend in mayonnaise, lemon juice, Worcestershire sauce, Tabasco sauce and green onions.

~ Pour into a lightly oiled 1½-quart mold and chill until firm.

YIELD: 8 SERVINGS

Oven-Roasted Beets with Balsamic Vinaigrette*

We love oven-roasted beets. Try them warm with some salt and pepper and a little butter if you wish. We have found that even those who say they don't like beets will enjoy this dish.

3	fresh medium beets
1	tablespoon olive oil
¼	cup balsamic vinegar
1	teaspoon Dijon mustard
¾	cup good quality olive oil
	Salt and pepper to taste

➤ Wash beets well, dry them and rub with 1 tablespoon olive oil. Place on a baking pan and bake in a 375-degree oven for 45 minutes to 1½ hours or until tender when pierced with a fork. I find that beets vary widely in the amount of time it takes them to cook—that probably has to do with how fresh they are.

➤ Remove from oven when tender, let cool and peel off skin with a sharp knife. Allow to cool completely, then cut into thin julienne strips.

➤ In a small bowl, combine vinegar and mustard. Whisk in ¾ cup olive oil, taste and add salt and pepper to your liking. Pour desired amount of dressing over beets and toss. You may not need to use all the dressing and you may want to add some more vinegar.

YIELD: 6 SERVINGS

Corn Casserole

2   *(16-ounce) cans cream-style corn*
6   *eggs*
1/4   *teaspoon seasoned salt*
2   *tablespoons butter*
1   *bunch green onions, finely chopped*
1   *cup heavy cream*
1   *cup fresh bread crumbs from stale*
       bread or cracker crumbs

- In a large bowl, combine corn and well-beaten eggs with seasoned salt.
- In a skillet, melt butter and sauté green onions until soft. Add to corn with cream and bread crumbs. Pour into well-greased casserole dish.
- Bake at 350 degrees for 1 hour or more or until firm.

YIELD: 8 SERVINGS

Eggplant and Smoked Oyster Casserole

I created this as a substitute for the scalloped oysters which I like to serve at Thanksgiving. We can't afford to do scalloped oysters on a buffet for 150 people, so we came up with this. I think it's pretty good.

1	large or 2 small eggplant, peeled, cubed
3	eggs
3	tablespoons butter
1	cup chopped onion
3/4	cup crumbled saltine crackers
5	ounces canned smoked oysters or smoked mussels, coarsely chopped
1/4	teaspoon freshly ground pepper
3/4	teaspoon dried oregano leaves
1/2	pound grated Swiss cheese

- Boil eggplant until tender. Drain excess moisture and mash with a fork.
- Mix eggs, butter, onion, cracker crumbs, oysters, pepper and oregano. Combine egg mixture with eggplant and blend thoroughly.
- Pour into greased baking dish and top with cheese. Bake, uncovered, for 30 to 45 minutes or until casserole is cooked throughout and browned on top.

YIELD: 12 SERVINGS

Black-Eyed Peas in
Tomato and Onion Sauce

1 cup black-eyed peas
4 cups cold water
½ cup light olive oil
1 medium onion, chopped
½ teaspoon crushed garlic
1¾ cups chopped seeded peeled tomatoes
Salt and pepper to taste
2 tablespoons finely chopped parsley

❧ Pick over peas. Wash peas and place in large pot with water. Don't overcrowd peas in pot. Cook over medium-high heat for 30 minutes, then test for doneness. If they are tender but firm and have no raw taste, drain and immediately run under cold water to stop cooking. Drain and set aside. If not done, cook for another 10 minutes, then test again.

❧ Heat a 9-inch skillet until hot, then add olive oil. Add the onion and sauté 1 minute. Then add garlic and tomatoes and cook slowly for 30 minutes. Stir often during cooking. Add black-eyed peas, mix well and season with salt and pepper. Cook gently for 10 minutes more, then add parsley. Spoon into a casserole and keep warm until serving time.

YIELD: 4 SERVINGS

Broiled Radicchio with Balsamic Vinegar*

2   *small heads radicchio*
1   *tablespoon olive oil*
4   *teaspoons balsamic vinegar*
      Salt to taste
      Freshly ground black pepper to taste

❧ Cut the heads of radicchio in half. Sprinkle the cut side of each piece of radicchio with olive oil.

❧ Preheat the broiler and place the radicchio halves on a pan under the heat source for 2 to 3 minutes until the top is slightly browned. The radicchio should be heated but still crisp.

❧ Drizzle a teaspoon or more of balsamic vinegar on each half and sprinkle with salt and pepper to taste. Serve as an appetizer, salad or vegetable.

YIELD: 4 SERVINGS

Holiday Spinach

We serve this easy spinach recipe on our Thanksgiving and Easter Buffets. Even spinach haters like it. We bake it in loaf pans a day ahead, then slice it cold and serve it at room temperature with a roasted red pepper sauce. It also works well baked in small ramekins or muffin cups.

2	tablespoons finely chopped green onions
1	tablespoon butter
1	(10-ounce) package frozen chopped spinach, thawed
1	egg, lightly beaten
1/4	cup half-and-half
2	tablespoons grated Parmesan cheese
3/4	cup bread crumbs
	Dash of salt
	Dash of nutmeg
	Dash of pepper

> Sauté the green onions in the butter in a skillet. Squeeze excess moisture from the spinach. Combine with the green onions, egg, half-and-half, Parmesan cheese, bread crumbs, salt, nutmeg and pepper in a food processor container. Process until well combined. Spoon into 6 well-greased ramekins or muffin cups.

> Bake at 350 degrees for 20 minutes or until firm in the center. Invert onto serving plate. Serve warm or at room temperature with Roasted Red Pepper Sauce (page 138).

> To serve a large crowd, double the recipe and bake in a 5x9-inch loaf pan for 45 minutes to 1 hour. Cool and slice before serving.

YIELD: 6 SERVINGS

Squash Gratiné

2 tablespoons olive oil

6 small yellow squash, thickly sliced on the diagonal

1 bunch green onions, chopped

2 cloves of garlic, finely chopped

1/4 teaspoon cayenne pepper

2 tablespoons soy sauce

4 Roma tomatoes, coarsely chopped
   Salt to taste

1/4 cup freshly grated Parmesan cheese
   Additional Parmesan cheese for top of casserole

1 heaping tablespoon Sour Cream

- Heat olive oil in skillet. Add squash, green onions, garlic, cayenne and soy sauce. Sauté until tender.

- Add tomatoes and salt. Sauté 1 or 2 minutes, tossing to combine well with squash. Remove from heat and stir in 1/4 cup Parmesan. *Sour cream*

- Pour into a shallow casserole dish, sprinkle top generously with additional Parmesan and broil briefly until browned on top. Serve immediately.

YIELD: 4 SERVINGS

Creole Sweet Potato Pone

We have been making this for Thanksgiving every year since we opened and it has evolved over the years. It is a lot of trouble, but well worth the effort.

4	(16-ounce) cans sweet potatoes
1/2	cup butter, melted
2	eggs, slightly beaten
1	teaspoon vanilla extract
2	teaspoons cinnamon
1/2	teaspoon allspice
1/4	teaspoon freshly grated nutmeg
1/4	teaspoon ground ginger
1/4	teaspoon salt
1/2	cup sugar
2	tablespoons brown sugar
1 1/2	teaspoons orange zest
1/2	cup fresh orange juice
1/4	teaspoon lemon zest
6	tablespoons flour
1	tablespoon baking powder
1/2	cup butter, softened
1	cup packed brown sugar
1/2	cup heavy cream
1	cup coarsely chopped walnuts

- Combine sweet potatoes with the next 13 ingredients. Refrigerate. May prepare sweet potatoes the day before. Day of serving stir in flour and baking powder.
- Spread into 9x13-inch baking dish and spread topping on top (see below).
- Bake at 350 degrees for 45 minutes to 1 hour or until set in center. Let stand for 15 minutes before serving.
- To prepare topping, combine 1/2 cup butter, 1 cup brown sugar and cream. Cook to 234 to 240 degrees on a candy thermometer, soft-boil stage; add walnuts. Cool and spread over sweet potatoes before baking.

YIELD: 12 SERVINGS

Broiled Tomatoes*

A quick and easy accompaniment to roast chicken or any grilled meat or fish.

6	Roma tomatoes
	Salt and pepper to taste
30	teaspoons creamed horseradish
	(available in gourmet section
	of most supermarkets)
30	tablespoons grated Parmesan cheese

⁊➤ Slice tomatoes into 5 slices each. Arrange tomato slices on a baking sheet. Sprinkle with salt and pepper. Spread with creamed horseradish and sprinkle with Parmesan.

⁊➤ Broil until cheese browns. Serve hot.

YIELD: 4 SERVINGS

Basil

Entrées

Grilled Marinated London Broil

4	large cloves of garlic, minced
1/4	cup balsamic vinegar
1/4	cup lemon juice
3	tablespoons Dijon mustard
1 1/2	tablespoons Worcestershire sauce
1	tablespoon soy sauce
1	teaspoon dried oregano
1	teaspoon dried basil
1	teaspoon dried thyme
1/2	teaspoon dried hot red pepper flakes
2/3	cup olive oil
2 1/2	pounds London broil

- In a bowl whisk together marinade ingredients until combined well.

- Put London broil in large resealable plastic bag and pour marinade over it. Seal bag, pressing out excess air, and set in a shallow dish. Marinate meat, chilled, overnight, turning bag once or twice.

- Remove meat from marinade and grill on an oiled rack about 4 inches over glowing coals for 9 to 10 minutes on each side, turning it once. Transfer meat to a cutting board and let stand for 10 minutes. Cut meat diagonally across the grain into thin slices.

YIELD: 6 SERVINGS

Roasted Beef Tenderloin

1	whole (3- to 4-pound) fillet of beef, trimmed
2	tablespoons salt
1	tablespoon black pepper
2	teaspoons celery salt
2	teaspoons onion salt
	Juice of 2 lemons
2/3	cup steak sauce
1/4	cup Worcestershire sauce
2	ounces paprika

❧ The day before or early in the day, wash fillet and pat dry. Rub salt into meat. Follow with black pepper, celery salt and onion salt, rubbing well so that the seasonings get into all crevices.

❧ In a small bowl, blend lemon juice, steak sauce and Worcestershire sauce together. Rub into meat. Set aside any extra sauce.

❧ Place fillet in shallow roasting pan and coat with paprika. Refrigerate for 8 to 10 hours.

❧ Preheat oven to 550 degrees. Pour the meat juices and any leftover sauce over the fillet. Roast, uncovered, at 550 degrees for 10 minutes. Reduce heat to 450 degrees and roast for 8 to 10 minutes per pound.

❧ Let the roast cool slightly before carving.

YIELD: 8 SERVINGS

Chicken Potpie

We serve this often to our conference groups for lunch and it's always a hit. Using boneless chicken breast makes this much easier to prepare than a traditional recipe with whole chicken.

1½	quarts chicken stock or canned broth
½	large onion, chopped
2½	stalks celery, chopped
2	large carrots, chopped
2	large potatoes, peeled, chopped
5	chicken breast halves without skin
4	ounces frozen peas
¾	cup frozen corn kernels
3	cups (or more) sifted flour
6	ounces butter
1½	cups milk
1½	cups self-rising flour

- Cook the first 6 ingredients in a saucepan until chicken and vegetables are tender. Add peas and corn. Drain liquid into another saucepan. Chop chicken.
- Thicken the liquid by whisking in 3 cups sifted flour very gradually. Cook over low heat until thick, stirring constantly and adding additional sifted flour if needed. Add the chicken and vegetables to the thick liquid. Pour into a 9x13-inch pan and let cool.
- Make the crust by heating butter until melted, stir in milk and whisk in 1½ cups self-rising flour. Spread batter on top of the cooled chicken.
- Bake at 375 degrees for 1 hour.

YIELD: 10 SERVINGS

Marinade for Grilled Chicken

1/4   cup fresh lemon juice
1   teaspoon chopped garlic
1   teaspoon kosher salt
1   teaspoon liquid smoke
1   teaspoon Worcestershire sauce
1/2   cup peanut oil

❧ Blend lemon juice, garlic, kosher salt, liquid smoke, Worcestershire sauce and peanut oil in blender.

❧ Pour over boneless chicken breasts or chicken pieces and marinate, refrigerated, for at least an hour but no more than 4 hours, as the lemon juice tends to cook the chicken it if marinates for too long.

❧ Drain the chicken, discarding the marinade. Cook the chicken on a hot grill until done to taste.

YIELD: 8 SERVINGS

Sage

Marinated Grilled Duck Breast with Sweet Cranberry Relish

2	cups vegetable oil
2	tablespoons minced garlic
2	tablespoons Worcestershire sauce
1/2	cup red wine
1	teaspoon dried thyme leaves
1	teaspoon dried basil leaves
1	teaspoon rosemary, fresh or dried
4	duck breasts (skin on)
	Sweet Cranberry Relish

 Combine oil, garlic, Worcestershire sauce, wine and herbs. Place duck in a single layer in a shallow pan, pour marinade over duck breasts and marinate overnight. On charcoal or gas grill, cook duck to medium-rare or desired doneness, remove and slice each breast diagonally into 4 pieces, fan out on serving plate and top with the Sweet Cranberry Relish.

YIELD: 4 SERVINGS

Sweet Cranberry Relish

2	cups dried cranberries
1	red onion
1	red bell pepper
1	green pepper
3	tablespoons olive oil
1	tablespoon sugar
1/4	cup apple cider vinegar
	Salt and pepper to taste

 Cover cranberries with water. Bring briefly to boil to rehydrate. Dice vegetables. Sauté lightly in olive oil. Add cranberries and liquid. Add sugar, vinegar, and salt and pepper. Continue to cook for 5 minutes. Serve relish at room temperature.

Smoked Turkey

———◦/◦/◦———

1	*whole raw turkey breast or whole turkey, fresh or frozen*
¼	*cup kosher salt*
¼	*cup vegetable oil*
1	*cup cider vinegar*
2	*tablespoons coarsely ground black pepper*
¼	*cup dried parsley*

੨► You can do this on any covered grill or smoker. If you have a rotisserie, use it. If you are using a grill without a rotisserie, spread the coals around the edge of the grill away from the meat. You can also put the turkey in an iron skillet or any roasting pan that you don't mind getting covered with black soot. (It will wash off.)

੨► Thaw frozen turkey thoroughly in refrigerator for several days. Wipe with damp paper towels inside and out.

੨► Combine salt, oil, vinegar, pepper and parsley. Rub turkey thoroughly all over with this mixture inside and out. You may need to make more marinade if cooking a whole turkey.

੨► Place in a covered grill or smoker and cook according to manufacturer's directions for your particular equipment. Let turkey cook for 1 hour, then begin basting with marinade every 20 minutes if using a grill, less often if using a smoker, until turkey is done.

YIELD: 8 SERVINGS

Honey-Roasted Rack of Lamb with Horseradish Mint Sauce

This was our original recipe for rack of lamb. Our current chef serves a different sauce, but I still like this one.

½	cup honey
¼	cup Worcestershire sauce
1	cup salad oil
4	(14-ounce) lamb racks
16	ounces apple-mint jelly
1	tablespoon horseradish
1	tablespoon cider vinegar
1	tablespoon chopped fresh mint

❧ In a large bowl, whisk together honey, Worcestershire sauce and oil.

❧ Place lamb in a large shallow pan, pour marinade over and let sit refrigerated for 6 hours or overnight. Wipe marinade from racks with a paper towel and if convenient sear racks for a couple of minutes on each side on a gas or electric grill. Watch carefully as the honey glaze burns easily. If grill is not available, skip this step.

❧ Remove from grill and place on a rack in a roasting pan in a 425-degree oven for 20 to 30 minutes or until desired degree of doneness is reached. Note: Flavor and tenderness is much better if meat is not cooked well-done. If a convection oven is available, use it and reduce cooking time by about ¼.

❧ To serve, let meat rest for about 5 minutes, then slice between each rack with a sharp knife. Arrange on platter and serve immediately with sauce on the side.

❧ Directions for sauce: In a saucepan, heat jelly until melted, stir in horseradish and vinegar. Cool and stir in chopped mint. Sauce will keep for 1 month refrigerated.

YIELD: 4 SERVINGS

Smoked Tomato and Onion Relish for Pork, Chicken or Fish

8	*fresh plum tomatoes, peeled, seeded*
1	*(2-inch) chunk mesquite or hickory wood*
1	*red onion*
1/4	*cup olive oil*
	Salt and pepper to taste
1/4	*cup balsamic or cider vinegar, warmed, mixed with 1 teaspoon Tabasco sauce*

❧ Cold-smoking the tomatoes: You will need a large roasting pan with a wire rack that will fit inside the pan and enough heavy-duty aluminum foil to cover the pan tightly.

❧ Place the peeled and seeded tomatoes on the rack in the pan, leaving a space about 4 inches in diameter in the center of the rack.

❧ Place the chunk of wood directly on the coals of an electric, gas or charcoal grill and leave it there until it is well charred and smoldering (about 5 minutes).

❧ With tongs, carefully move the piece of wood to the space in the center of the pan and very quickly cover the pan with the foil, sealing it tightly. Let the tomatoes sit for 30 minutes. If a more intense smoked flavor is desired you may repeat the process. Chop coarsely and set aside.

❧ Grilling the onion: Peel and slice the onion into ½-inch rings. Carefully toss the onion in the oil and seasonings, keeping rings intact, and cook on the grill until they are charred (about 10 minutes). Remove them from the grill and chop coarsely. Add the smoked tomatoes and the heated vinegar. Taste and add more salt and pepper if desired.

❧ Wonderful on top of pork tenderloin, boneless chicken breast or a baked fish such as grouper. Will keep several days in refrigerator.

YIELD: 6 SERVINGS

Nancy's Roast Pork

—◦◦◦—

1	*head fresh garlic*
1	*(2½- to 3-pound) boneless pork loin roast*
1	*teaspoon coarsely ground black pepper*
¼	*cup all-purpose flour*
1	*teaspoon finely chopped fresh rosemary leaves*
1	*teaspoon salt*
¼	*cup olive oil*
	Salt and pepper to taste

- Preheat oven to 500 degrees.

- Peel garlic and cut cloves into slivers—you'll need about 20.

- With a sharp knife, pierce roast about 1 inch deep at 1½-inch intervals all over, inserting slivers of garlic into each slit as you go. Don't make all the slits and then try to go back because you won't be able to see them.

- Pat 1 teaspoon pepper evenly over roast. Combine flour, rosemary and 1 teaspoon salt and rub into roast, dusting off excess flour.

- In a heavy cast-iron skillet or Dutch oven, sear roast in the olive oil, turning to brown evenly on all sides. Remove from heat and add enough water to cover bottom of pan by ½ inch.

- Place in oven at 500 degrees for 15 minutes, then lower heat to 350 degrees and roast for about 20 minutes per pound or until meat registers 160 degrees on an instant-read meat thermometer. Check roast periodically and add more water to pan if needed.

- Remove roast from pan and make gravy by whisking a few tablespoons flour into the drippings. Season gravy with salt and pepper to taste.

YIELD: 6 SERVINGS

Honey-Glazed Baked Ham

We use this method for our Thanksgiving hams. It gives the ham a wonderful flavor. Nobody will believe you started with an already-cooked ham.

1   (6-pound) fully cooked boneless ham
4   sticks cinnamon
12   whole cloves (optional)
1   tablespoon fresh lemon juice or
        part orange juice
1/4 cup brown sugar
1/4 cup honey
2   tablespoons Dijon mustard
1   teaspoon ground cloves

- Place ham and cinnamon sticks in a large pot. Cover ham with water and bring to a boil. Reduce heat and simmer very slowly for 1 hour.
- Turn off heat and let ham sit on stove until liquid cools, about an hour. Remove ham from liquid and dry with paper towels.
- If desired slice crisscross cuts on top and sides of ham and stud with whole cloves.
- Combine lemon juice, brown sugar, honey, Dijon mustard and ground cloves.
- Place ham in a shallow baking pan and brush with glaze mixture.
- Bake ham in a low oven (275 to 300 degrees) for 1 to 1½ hours or until nicely browned, basting with glaze every 20 minutes. If ham is browning too fast, lower oven temperature.
- Remember ham is already cooked; you are just glazing it.

YIELD: 12 SERVINGS

Salmon Cakes

1½	pounds fresh salmon, poached or steamed
2	cups coarsely crumbled saltine crackers, divided
1	teaspoon paprika
½	cup finely chopped green onions
¼	cup finely chopped fresh parsley
½	teaspoon salt
¼	teaspoon black pepper
2	large eggs, lightly beaten
¼	cup vegetable oil

- Remove skin and bones from salmon and crumble coarsely.
- Add 1 cup of cracker crumbs and all other ingredients except oil and toss gently to mix without turning mixture to mush.
- Shape into 8 patties. Place remaining crumbs on plate and dredge patties in crumbs. Chill for about 1 hour before cooking.
- Heat oil in large nonstick skillet. Cook patties for about 2½ minutes on each side or until golden brown. Drain on paper towels.
- Serve with tartar sauce.

YIELD: 4 SERVINGS

Salmon in Parchment*

≈≈≈

6 ounces fresh salmon
  Salt and pepper to taste
½ cup julienned vegetables
    (squash, zucchini and onion)
1 tablespoon butter
1 tablespoon white wine
1 tablespoon lemon juice
½ tablespoon freshly chopped dill

- Place ingredients in order listed in center of ½ parchment sheet.
- Bring ends of sheet together in center over fish and fold towards fish in 3 to 4 folds, forming a packet. Pinch ends of packet together tightly and fold towards fish.
- Bake in oven at 400 degrees for 15 to 18 minutes or until fish is done.

YIELD: 1 SERVING

Japanese Marinade for Salmon

≈≈≈

1 cup sake
½ cup Japanese or Korean soy sauce
¼ cup balsamic vinegar

- Combine sake, soy sauce and balsamic vinegar in a bowl.
- Add fresh whole salmon or salmon fillets to bowl and marinate for 30 minutes.
- Grill or bake as desired, brushing with additional sauce if you wish.

YIELD: 4 SERVINGS

Trout Pecan

—◦◦◦—

Everybody loves our trout. It's a very simple dish and I think the lime juice really complements the flavor of the trout. New chefs keep trying to get fancy with the preparation. Every now and then a guest will say "Your trout isn't the same anymore." That's when I have to go back to the kitchen and remind them how it's supposed to be prepared.

½	cup chopped pecans
4	(6- to 7-ounce) fresh rainbow trout fillets
2	cups Our Coating Mix (page 138)
½	cup butter
1	to 2 fresh limes, halved
1	tablespoon minced fresh herbs

➤ Toast pecans for about 5 minutes in a 350-degree oven and set aside. Turn oven to 325 degrees.

➤ Dredge fillets in coating mix. In a large nonstick skillet heat enough butter to just cover bottom of skillet. When very hot, add trout fillets skin side up. If your skillet isn't large enough to hold all the trout without crowding, do this in 2 steps. Reduce heat to medium and cook trout on flesh side for about 5 minutes or until trout is nicely browned.

➤ Transfer the fish browned side up to an ovenproof baking dish and continue cooking the rest of the fish, adding more butter if needed. If butter in skillet starts looking burned, wipe out skillet and add more butter.

➤ Squeeze lime juice over each fillet; sprinkle with the herbs and the toasted pecans. Place in oven and bake for about 5 minutes or until fillets flake easily with a fork. Serve with an extra wedge of lime.

YIELD: 4 SERVINGS

Grilled Tuna with Orange Ginger Sauce*

1   cup fresh orange juice
1   teaspoon Dijon mustard
6   tablespoons extra-virgin olive oil
2½   teaspoons minced fresh ginger
     Salt and pepper to taste
4   (6-ounce) top-quality fresh tuna
         steaks

2➤ In a small heavy saucepan, bring orange juice to a boil and reduce over medium heat to about ⅓ cup.

2➤ Turn heat to low and whisk in mustard and oil. Stir in ginger and season with salt and pepper. Remove from heat and set aside.

2➤ Sauce will keep in refrigerator for 1 to 2 days; let come to room temperature before serving with tuna. Grill tuna to desired doneness and drizzle with sauce.

2➤ This sauce is also good over a spinach salad.

YIELD: 4 SERVINGS

Jeff's Crab Cakes

I think these are the best crab cakes I have ever had. Jeff is our current chef and this is his recipe.

1	pound fresh crab meat (Jeff uses lump blue crab)
1/2	cup finely diced celery
1/2	cup finely diced red onion
1/2	cup finely diced red and green bell pepper
1	cup dry bread crumbs
1 1/2	cups mayonnaise
1	tablespoon Dijon mustard
1	tablespoon chopped parsley
2	teaspoons Old Bay seasoning
	Salt and pepper to taste
1/2	cup dry bread crumbs
1/2	cup biscuit mix or flour
1/2	cup olive oil
2	tablespoons finely chopped fresh dill, or 1 tablespoon dried dill
1/2	cup white wine
1 1/2	cups heavy cream

❧ Combine crab, celery, onion, bell pepper, bread crumbs, mayonnaise, mustard, parsley and Old Bay seasoning. Taste mixture and add salt and pepper if desired.

❧ Form into 8 patties. Combine bread crumbs and biscuit mix or flour and coat crab cakes lightly. Refrigerate until just before serving.

❧ In a large skillet, heat enough olive oil to cover bottom of pan. Oil should be very hot—almost smoking. Carefully add several crab cakes to pan without crowding and cook on each side for about 2 minutes or until golden brown.

- As each cake is browned, remove it from the skillet and place on a baking pan. Continue until all cakes are browned.

- Bake crab cakes in a 400-degree oven for 10 to 12 minutes or until heated through. While crab cakes are baking, prepare Creamy Dill Sauce.

- Creamy Dill Sauce: In a saucepan combine dill and white wine and cook over medium heat until wine is reduced by half.

- Add heavy cream and continue to cook, stirring until sauce is desired consistency.

- Season to taste, and drizzle over crab cakes before serving.

YIELD: 4 SERVINGS

Dill

Seafood Risotto

—⟨℘℘⟩—

Bobby and I both adore risotto. This is the way I make it. It's somewhat different from the recipe Jeff has contributed, which is the one currently on our menu. I especially like to do this one when we're at the beach and can get really fresh seafood. You can vary the seafood; crab or lobster or crayfish would be great or just use all shrimp.

5	cups Easy Shellfish Stock, heated (page 128)
1	tablespoon finely chopped onion
5	tablespoons olive oil
2	teaspoons finely chopped garlic
2	tablespoons chopped parsley
2	cups raw Italian arborio rice
1/3	cup dry white wine
1/4	teaspoon saffron threads (optional)
1/2	pound peeled and deveined shrimp
1/2	pound scallops, cut into pieces if large
	Salt and pepper to taste

- Bring the 5 cups stock (and water if needed) to a slow steady simmer in a separate saucepan.
- In a heavy-bottomed casserole or Dutch oven, sauté the onion in olive oil over medium heat. When translucent, add the garlic and sauté until it colors lightly.
- Add the parsley, stir, then add the rice and stir until it is well coated with oil. Sauté lightly for a few moments and then add the wine and saffron.

- Cook over low heat. When the wine has almost evaporated, begin adding the simmering stock about ½ cup at a time. Continue adding stock every few minutes as needed, stirring constantly to keep rice from sticking. It is very important that the rice not stick.

- Meanwhile in a nonstick skillet with a little oil, quickly sauté the shrimp and scallops over high heat until they are just barely done (about 2 to 3 minutes). Set aside.

- After the rice has cooked for about 15 minutes, taste a kernel. It should be still hard in the center but beginning to soften on the outside. At this point you are about 5 minutes away from serving. Add salt and pepper to taste and add the seafood. Continue cooking as before, adding broth as needed until rice is done — tender but al dente — still firm to the bite.

- To make ahead: Cook rice to halfway point (outside is almost tender but it's still very firm in the center). Allow to dry out, then remove from heat and spread on a cold platter. About 15 minutes before serving, melt 1 tablespoon butter or heat oil in a casserole. Add the rice and stir, coating it well with butter. Meanwhile bring broth back to simmer and resume cooking it in the same way until done.

YIELD: 6 SERVINGS

Easy Shellfish Stock

2   tablespoons vegetable oil
2   cups coarsely chopped onions,
        peel and all
1   cup chopped carrots, not peeled
1   cup chopped celery with leaves
4   cloves of garlic, unpeeled
2   cups dry white wine
2   bay leaves
1   teaspoon dried thyme leaves
6   whole peppercorns
     Shells from 5 pounds of shrimp
2   quarts water

- Place oil and vegetables in a large stockpot and cook slowly over medium heat for about 20 minutes or until vegetables are lightly browned.
- Add wine, seasonings, shrimp shells and 2 quarts of water. Simmer stock for about 20 more minutes. Strain stock and refrigerate or freeze until needed.

YIELD: 2 QUARTS STOCK

Seared Scallop and Bacon Risotto

This recipe comes from our current chef, Jeff McKenna, and is served as an appetizer in our dining room. It is rather rich, and if serving it as a first course, follow it with a salad and a very light entrée—European style.

4	thickly sliced smoked bacon strips
1	small Vidalia or other mild onion
10	ounces arborio rice
1½	quarts chicken broth or stock
1	teaspoon finely chopped fresh oregano
1	teaspoon finely chopped fresh basil
	Salt and pepper to taste
1	pound fresh scallops (any size)
2	tablespoons olive oil
½	cup half-and-half (optional)

➤ Chop bacon into ¼-inch pieces. Fry in a heavy-bottomed pot large enough to hold all the ingredients until bacon begins to render its fat and becomes crisp. Dice the onion, add it to the skillet and cook until it is translucent. Stir the rice into the pot with the bacon and onion. Cook rice, stirring for 1 or 2 minutes.

➤ At this point Jeff says to add enough stock to cover rice by 1 inch and cook until just barely tender, adding more stock if needed. The true Italian way would be to add the stock by 1-cup increments, stirring after each addition until most of the liquid is absorbed, continuing this process until the rice is almost tender. Either way, after about 15 minutes, test a kernel of rice between your teeth; when it is soft on the outside but still fairly firm in the center, it's time to season the rice with the herbs, salt and pepper, and to quickly sear the scallops.

➤ In another skillet, heat 2 tablespoons olive oil until it is smoking and quickly sear the scallops for just 1 or 2 minutes. Naturally it will take longer to cook large-size scallops, but the tiny ones will cook in less than 1 minute.

➤ Add the scallops to the risotto and continue to cook if needed until the rice is done, adding the half-and-half if desired to make it extra creamy. I think if you cook the rice the Italian way, it becomes more creamy and you don't need the half-and-half. Properly cooked risotto rice should still be a little firm in the center—al dente.

YIELD: 4 SERVINGS

Low Country Shrimp and Gravy

Lobster base is a concentrated extract similar to a bouillon cube. It is not easy to find but is becoming more available at some gourmet stores in Atlanta such as Harris Teeter and Harry's Farmers Market. Jonathan Dean, a former chef, and I invented this several years ago. Shrimp and Gravy is a traditional dish of the South Carolina and Georgia coast, and versions of it are served today in many restaurants in that area. This is ours.

½	red bell pepper, diced
½	green bell pepper, diced
½	cup diced Vidalia onion
3	tablespoons butter
3	tablespoons flour
1	quart water
1	tablespoon lobster base or any seafood base
2	tablespoons Worcestershire sauce
1	teaspoon Tabasco sauce, or to taste
	Salt to taste
2	tablespoons butter
2	pounds large peeled and deveined shrimp

➢ In a heavy skillet, sauté peppers and onion in butter for 1 to 2 minutes. Sprinkle flour over vegetables and cook, stirring over low heat for at least 5 minutes. Watch carefully and don't let the mixture get too brown.

➢ Gradually whisk in the water, stir in seafood base, Worcestershire sauce, Tabasco sauce and seasoning to taste, and cook until thickened.

➢ Sauté shrimp in a large nonstick skillet over high heat just until shrimp turn pink. Stir the shrimp into the gravy just before serving and reheat.

➢ Serve over Fried Parmesan Grits (page 131).

YIELD: 4 SERVINGS

Fried Parmesan Grits

We serve these with our Low Country Shrimp Gravy, but they would be good for breakfast also. The addition of cream to the grits helps them to hold together better. I have made them with water or broth also, but they don't hold up as well in frying. Sometimes I'm embarrassed by all the fat we use in our recipes, but I have to remind myself that people don't come here to eat diet food, they come here to eat GOOD FOOD!

4   cups milk
2   cups half-and-half, or 1 cup
           half-and-half and 1 cup
           heavy cream
1/4   pound butter
1 1/2 cups quick (not instant) grits
1/2   cup finely grated Parmesan cheese
1   shake Tabasco sauce
         Salt and pepper to taste
1/2   cup dry bread crumbs
1/2   cup biscuit mix or all-purpose flour
         Vegetable oil for frying

- Bring milk, half-and-half and butter to a boil in a large heavy-bottomed saucepan. (Jeff actually uses 1 cup heavy cream and 1 cup half-and-half.)
- Add grits and Parmesan cheese and cook until very thick. Add Tabasco sauce, salt and pepper as needed when grits have cooked about half way. (The butter and Parmesan contain salt so you may not need much.)
- Pour the grits into one or more loaf pans, filling completely. Chill the grits overnight. Before frying, remove grits from pan and slice 1/2 inch thick, then cut into interesting shapes with a knife or biscuit cutter if desired. Jeff uses circles and half moons.
- Combine bread crumbs and biscuit mix or flour, coat grit cakes lightly with breading and either deep-fry or pan-sauté in oil until golden brown. These can be made up to 1/2 hour in advance and kept warm in the oven at a low heat setting.

YIELD: 4 SERVINGS

Shrimp Kabobs

A popular item on our original menu. I had forgotten about them until I started looking through old recipe files.

6	*jumbo shrimp, peeled, deveined, tails on*
3	*(1-inch) pieces andouille sausage*
2	*mushrooms*
2	*(1-inch) pieces green or red bell pepper*
2	*(1-inch) pieces onion*
	Vegetable oil to coat
	Cajun Seasoning

❧ Thread a 12-inch skewer with shrimp and sausage. Thread another skewer with the mushrooms, bell pepper and onion.

❧ Brush each kabob with oil and sprinkle with Cajun Seasoning (page 139).

❧ Grill kabobs, turning once every 5 minutes until done.

YIELD: 1 SERVING

Marinara with Roasted Eggplant

26	ounces canned diced tomatoes
2	teaspoons fresh chopped garlic
1/2	teaspoon red pepper flakes
1/2	pound eggplant
	Salt to taste
1/4	cup olive oil
	Freshly cooked pasta, any kind
	Freshly grated Parmesan cheese

❧ Process diced tomatoes in food processor briefly. Combine tomatoes, garlic and red pepper in medium saucepan. Simmer for about 30 minutes.

❧ Slice eggplant into 1/2-inch rounds; salt slices on both sides, let set for 30 minutes, then blot with paper towel. Cut eggplant into 1/2x3-inch sticks.

❧ Coat a shallow baking pan with olive oil; add eggplant and toss to coat with oil. Roast at 400 degrees for 20 minutes or until tender. Add eggplant to sauce and simmer a few minutes.

❧ Serve over pasta with Parmesan cheese.

YIELD: 4 SERVINGS

Vegetarian Lasagne

⟨∽∾∽⟩

Jeff makes wonderful fresh spinach pasta which I love to use for this dish. Some specialty food markets sell fresh pasta, or just use the dried kind. I think this is the best lasagna I have ever eaten — forget the meat, this is divine!

1	medium eggplant
1	teaspoon kosher salt
½	cup olive oil, divided
1	green bell pepper, cut into strips
1	red bell pepper, cut into strips
1	large onion, cut into strips
12	ounces fresh mushrooms, sliced
8	ounces lasagne noodles, fresh if possible
	Marinara Sauce
¼	cup freshly grated Parmesan cheese
1½	cups Basic White Sauce or Béchamel (page 137)
5	ounces mild fresh goat cheese
½	cup fresh basil leaves, julienne cut
8	ounces mozzarella cheese, grated

- ❧ Slice eggplant into rounds ¼ inch thick. Sprinkle with kosher salt and let drain in a colander for 1 hour. Wipe off the salt and pat dry.

- ❧ Arrange eggplant in a single layer on a flat baking sheet; brush with olive oil.

- ❧ Bake at 350 degrees for about 20 minutes or until tender. Set aside.

- ❧ Heat 2 tablespoons olive oil in a skillet and sauté the peppers and onion over medium heat for about 10 minutes or until tender but not browned. Remove the peppers and onion and set aside.

- ❧ Add another tablespoon of oil and sauté the mushrooms for about 5 minutes or until cooked. Remove the mushrooms and set aside.

- ❧ Cook the dried lasagne according to package directions in a large pot of boiling water just until barely tender. Drain, rinse with cold water and drain again.

- If you are cooking fresh lasagne for the first time, you might want to get some instructions because it cooks very quickly and getting it out of the pot and drained without having it get overcooked or all tucked together can be tricky, but it's well worth the effort.
- In a 9x13-inch baking dish, spread a small amount of the marinara sauce. Arrange half of the cooked lasagne noodles over the sauce, then add the peppers, onion, mushrooms and eggplant in layers.
- Combine the Parmesan cheese with the white sauce and spoon half of it over the vegetables. Crumble the goat cheese over the white sauce and sprinkle with half of the basil.
- Top with more marinara sauce and remaining lasagne. Spread the rest of the white sauce over the lasagne and sprinkle with the remaining basil. Top with the rest of the marinara sauce and the mozzarella.
- Cover with foil and bake for 30 minutes, uncover and continue baking for about 15 minutes or until browned and bubbling.
- Let sit for about 15 minutes before serving.

YIELD: 6 SERVINGS

Marinara Sauce

26	ounces canned diced tomatoes
2	teaspoons fresh chopped garlic
1/2	teaspoon red pepper flakes

- Process diced tomatoes in food processor briefly. Combine tomatoes, garlic and red pepper in medium saucepan. Simmer for about 30 minutes. May substitute 3 cups bottled sauce.

Summer Supper Pasta*

This summer garden pasta comes from my good friend, Phyllis Kennedy who now lives in Montgomery, Alabama. She is one of the best cooks I know and has contributed several great recipes to this book. This really isn't a recipe with exact ingredients. It's an idea of a wonderful way to enjoy the bounty from your garden, or from the farmers' market, in midsummer. Vary the ingredients and the quantities to suit your taste.

4	ripe tomatoes, home grown if possible
1	cucumber
1	bell pepper
2	green onions
3	radishes (optional)
2	tablespoons chopped fresh herbs (basil, oregano, marjoram, thyme, etc.)
1	tablespoon olive oil
	Salt and pepper to taste
1	pound fresh or excellent-quality dried fettuccini or other pasta
1	cup (or more) freshly grated Parmesan cheese

- Peel and chop all the vegetables as you prefer—sliced or diced, etc., keeping as much juice as possible from the tomatoes.
- Place the vegetables in a large bowl, add the chopped fresh herbs, olive oil and salt and pepper to taste. Marinate for several hours at room temperature.
- Cook pasta al dente, drain and toss with generous amount of Parmesan cheese.
- Make a nest of hot pasta on each plate, with a depression in the center, and spoon vegetables into center, using a slotted spoon to eliminate extra juice. Enjoy!

YIELD: 4 SERVINGS

Basic White Sauce or Béchamel

This sauce is a staple of Southern cooking. It derives from the classic French Béchamel and has many variations. You can use stock or broth of any kind, part wine, part or all cream. To make a cheese sauce, add grated cheese of your choosing to the hot sauce and stir until smooth.

¼	cup butter
¼	cup flour
2	cups milk
	Dash of cayenne pepper
½	teaspoon salt

- In a heavy-bottomed saucepan, melt the butter. Remove pan from heat and whisk in the flour, mixing as well as possible before returning pan to heat. Return to stove and cook mixture over low heat for 2 minutes, whisking constantly.

- Gradually whisk in milk, whisking constantly to keep mixture from lumping. Increase heat some and keep whisking until mixture thickens. Add seasonings.

- Taste and correct seasonings. If the sauce has lumps of flour in it, strain to remove.

YIELD: 2 SERVINGS

Roasted Red Pepper Sauce

14	ounces canned roasted red peppers, well drained
1/4	cup heavy cream
1/4	teaspoon salt
1/2	teaspoon Texas Pete hot sauce

- Purée peppers in food processor until smooth.
- Add cream, salt and hot sauce and season to taste.
- Serve with Holiday Spinach (page 105).

YIELD: 12 SERVINGS

Our Coating Mix

This is the coating mix we use for our trout. I don't know why it works so well. It defies the laws of good cooking in that you shouldn't use a flour with a leavening agent for a breading mix, but rules are made to be broken, and this mixture makes the best breading for fried foods that we have ever found.

| 1 | cup seasoned bread crumbs or crushed croutons |
| 3 | cups Bisquick baking mix |

- Thoroughly combine bread crumbs and biscuit mix.
- Store in airtight container.

YIELD: 4 CUPS

Glen-Ella Springs

Spiced Cranberry Sauce

1 package fresh cranberries
1 cup water
1⅓ cups (or more) sugar
¼ teaspoon grated orange zest
½ teaspoon cinnamon
¼ teaspoon ground allspice
¼ teaspoon ground cloves

➺ Place cranberries, water, sugar, orange zest, cinnamon, allspice and cloves in a large heavy pot.
➺ Simmer briskly until it reaches sauce consistency.
➺ Taste and add more sugar and spices as desired.

YIELD: 8 SERVINGS

Cajun Seasoning

2 tablespoons salt
1 tablespoon granulated garlic powder
1 tablespoon black pepper
2 teaspoons cayenne
1 tablespoon dried thyme
1 tablespoon dried oregano
½ cup paprika
1 tablespoon granulated onion powder

➺ Combine salt, garlic powder, black pepper, cayenne, thyme, oregano, paprika and onion powder in a bowl and mix well. Rub mixture on fish or pork before grilling or use for blackened fish and to season shrimp kabobs.

YIELD: 1 CUP

Apple Chutney

1/4	cup fresh lemon juice
	Dash of granulated garlic
3	cups coarsely chopped peeled apples
1	cup packed brown sugar
1/4	cup apple schnapps
3/4	cup chopped dates
1 1/2	teaspoons grated fresh ginger
3/4	teaspoon salt
1	dash of cayenne pepper
1	cup cider vinegar

❧ Combine lemon juice, granulated garlic, chopped apples, brown sugar, apple schnapps, dates, ginger, salt, cayenne pepper and cider vinegar in medium saucepan and simmer until fruit is tender.

❧ Process briefly in food processor, leaving slightly chunky.

❧ Serve with ham, roast or grilled pork, or grilled chicken.

YIELD: 6 SERVINGS

Desserts and Other Sweets

Nut and Berry Bark

This candy is beautiful tied in clear, sealable plastic bags for Christmas gifts.

1½   cups shelled raw unsalted pistachios
1½   cups dried cranberries
1¼   pounds white chocolate, finely chopped

- Preheat oven to 350 degrees. Place pistachios in a cake pan and bake for 10 minutes, stirring occasionally. Don't overcook, or they will lose their bright green color. Remove from oven, cool completely.

- Place a steamer basket in a medium saucepan with ½ inch of water; bring to a boil. Place cranberries in basket, cover and steam until soft and moist (3 to 4 minutes). Remove basket and blot berries dry with paper towel. Cool completely. Reduce heat of water and keep the water at a simmer.

- Place ¾ of the chocolate in a heat-proof bowl and set over the simmering water. Using a rubber spatula, stir occasionally until about ⅔ melted (about 4 minutes). Remove the bowl from the heat and add the rest of the chocolate. Stir until completely melted. Cool to 83 degrees, stirring occasionally.

- Reserve 2 tablespoons each of cranberries and greenest pistachios. With a rubber spatula, stir nuts and berries into the chocolate. Scrape mixture onto a large baking sheet lined with parchment paper. Spread to about ⅜ inch thick. Scatter reserved nuts and berries over the chocolate.

- Refrigerate until hardened (20 to 30 minutes). Break bark into large pieces. May be stored in an airtight container for up to 1 week.

YIELD: 1½ POUNDS

Chocolate Temptation Cake

1	pound butter, softened
2	cups sugar
¼	cup apricot preserves
¼	cup crème de cassis
12	eggs
1	pound semisweet chocolate, melted
4	cups blanched almonds, finely ground
1	cup soft fresh bread crumbs

Beat butter and sugar until light. Add preserves and crème de cassis to sugar mixture and beat. Add eggs 4 at a time. Stir in last 3 ingredients. Grease 8-inch cake pans, line with parchment paper then grease again. Bake in 375-degree oven for 25 minutes. Cool for 15 minutes. Invert onto rack to cool. Sprinkle top with confectioners' sugar. Serve with Vanilla or Amaretto Custard Sauce (page 159).

YIELD: 4 CAKES

Joe's Mom's Raisin Pecan Cake

1	cup butter, softened
2	cups packed brown sugar
6	eggs
4	cups flour
2	pounds white raisins
4	cups chopped pecans

Combine butter, brown sugar, eggs, flour, white raisins and pecans in a bowl. Pour into tube pan or 2 loaf pans. Bake at 275 degrees for 2 hours.

YIELD: 16 SERVINGS

Molten Chocolate Cake

Our favorite new chocolate dessert, like a soufflé with a soft chocolate center—and so simple to do.

½	pound semisweet chocolate, chopped
½	pound unsalted butter
4	eggs
4	egg yolks
½	cup sugar
7	tablespoons all-purpose flour

- Butter and flour eight 5- to 6-ounce ovenproof custard cups or ramekins.
- Melt chocolate and butter over hot water in a double boiler; cool slightly.
- Beat eggs, yolks and sugar with electric mixer on medium-high until pale yellow (about 10 minutes). Reduce speed and add flour gradually. Add melted chocolate and beat until glossy (5 minutes). Pour mixture evenly into prepared cups.
- Bake at 325 degrees for 12 minutes or until set around edges but centers still move slightly. While still warm, turn out of custard cups upside down onto plate or serve in ramekins. Dust with confectioners' sugar and serve immediately over Vanilla Custard Sauce (page 159) if desired.
- To make ahead, fill ramekins and refrigerate up to 6 hours; add about 5 more minutes to baking time.

YIELD: 8 SERVINGS

White Chocolate Macadamia Nut Cheesecake

We adapted this from a recipe given to me by my good friend Sandy Wilbanks and it is a winner. Note that we cook ours at a temperature of 350 degrees, but that may be too hot for some other ovens. If cheesecake seems to be browning on top too much, turn down temperature to 325 degrees and cover top with foil if needed. Cakes may still jiggle slightly, but will firm up when chilled.

10	ounces vanilla wafer crumbs
2	ounces butter, melted
28	ounces cream cheese, softened
1	cup sugar
6	eggs
1	tablespoon vanilla extract
10	ounces premium quality white chocolate, chopped
1	cup macadamia nuts, coarsely chopped
5	ounces cream cheese, softened
3/4	cup sour cream
1/4	cup sugar

❧ Grease an 8- or 9-inch springform pan. Combine crumbs and melted butter until they stick together. Spread mixture evenly in pan for crust.

❧ Beat softened cream cheese in mixer until light. Add sugar, beat well. Add eggs, 1 at a time, mixing well. Stir in vanilla, white chocolate and nuts. Line outside of pan with foil same as for Pumpkin Cheesecake (page 146). Pour mixture halfway up the side of the pan. Bake at 350 degrees for 90 minutes. Turn off oven and let cheesecake remain in oven 1 more hour with door closed.

❧ Blend remaining ingredients until smooth.

❧ Spread over cooled cheesecake and refrigerate overnight.

YIELD: 8 SERVINGS

Pumpkin Cheesecake

—•o/o/o•—

1½	ounces margarine
1	cup graham cracker crumbs
⅓	cup chopped almonds
½	teaspoon cinnamon
2	pounds cream cheese, softened
4	eggs
1¾	cups sugar
1	cup pumpkin
2	teaspoons maple flavoring
1	teaspoon cinnamon
½	teaspoon nutmeg
½	teaspoon ginger

➤ Melt margarine and combine with graham cracker crumbs, almonds and cinnamon. Spread on bottom of 9-inch springform pan. Bake for 5 minutes at 325 degrees in convection oven.

➤ In electric mixer bowl, combine softened cream cheese, eggs, sugar, pumpkin, maple flavoring and spices. All ingredients should be at room temperature; if cream cheese is cold, batter will be lumpy. Mix until smooth. Pour into springform pan.

➤ Cut a sheet of heavy-duty (or use double thickness) aluminum foil large enough to come halfway up the side of the springform pan. Fit foil tightly around the pan. Place pan inside another larger baking pan and pour in 1 inch of boiling water. Place in oven and bake for 1½ hours at 350 degrees. Turn off oven and leave in oven with door closed for 1 hour. Remove from oven. Chill overnight.

➤ Decorate with toasted sliced almonds and whipped cream.

YIELD: 8 TO 10 SERVINGS

Lou's Chocolate Chip Cookies

Our baker, Lou Davis once owned a cookie company in Atlanta called Lulabelle's Gourmet Cookies. This was her favorite cookie.

1	pound butter
1/2	pound dark brown sugar
1 1/4	cups sugar
3	eggs
1 1/2	teaspoons vanilla extract
6	cups all-purpose flour
2 1/2	teaspoons baking powder
1	teaspoon salt
4	cups chocolate chips
1 1/4	cups chopped pecans
2	cups rolled oats

- Cream butter and sugars together. Add eggs and vanilla.
- Combine flour, baking powder and salt and add slowly to wet mixture.
- Stir in chips and pecans.
- Scoop dough into 24 balls using an ice cream scoop. Freeze unbaked dough on a cookie sheet and then pack into sealable plastic bags. Remove balls from freezer, thaw and bake as needed.
- Bake at 350 degrees for 8 minutes.
- For White Chocolate Chip Macadamia Nut Cookies, replace dark brown sugar with light brown sugar; chocolate chips with white chocolate morsels; pecans with macadamia nuts. Omit oats.

YIELD: 24 SERVINGS

Oatmeal Raisin Cookies

These cookies really do call for 3 pounds of oats. They are a really good old-fashioned oatmeal cookie.

1¼	pounds butter
3½	cups packed brown sugar
3	large eggs
3	tablespoons honey
1	tablespoon vanilla extract
1	tablespoon cinnamon
1½	teaspoons salt
4	cups all-purpose flour
3	pounds whole rolled oats (14 cups)
8	ounces raisins
8	ounces coarsely chopped walnuts or pecans

- Preheat oven to 350 degrees.
- Cream butter and brown sugar with electric mixer until smooth. Add eggs, honey, vanilla, cinnamon and salt and mix until smooth and creamy.
- Transfer this mixture to a large mixing bowl and add the flour and the oats, working them in with a large wooden spoon or with your hands until well combined. Add the raisins and walnuts and mix until evenly distributed.
- Shape the dough into large 3-inch balls. Place balls 1 at a time onto the baking sheet and press into 5- to 6-inch flat cookies.
- Bake cookies for 15 minutes for a soft chewy cookie, or about 5 minutes longer for a more crisp cookie. This will depend on your oven and whether you like them soft or well-browned.

YIELD: 24 SERVINGS

Peanut Butter Cookies

2½ cups flour
1 teaspoon salt
2 teaspoons cinnamon
1 teaspoon baking soda
1 cup butter, softened
1 cup packed brown sugar
1 cup sugar
1 cup creamy peanut butter
2 eggs
2 teaspoons vanilla extract

❧ Sift dry ingredients. Cream butter, sugars, peanut butter, eggs and vanilla for 2 minutes. Fold dry ingredients into creamed mixture.

❧ If not baking right away, roll dough into 20 balls, place balls on cookie sheet and freeze, then pack frozen balls into sealable plastic bags. Thaw before baking.

❧ Flatten slightly before baking. Bake in 350-degree oven for about 10 minutes.

YIELD: 20 SERVINGS

Fennel

Our Best Brownies

————— ꜱꜱꜱ —————

¾   cup all-purpose flour
¼   teaspoon baking soda
¾   cup sugar
⅓   cup butter or margarine
2   tablespoons water
1   (12-ounce) package semisweet
      chocolate chips
1   teaspoon vanilla extract
2   large eggs
½   cup chopped pecans

- Preheat oven to 325 degrees.
- Grease and flour a 9x9-inch baking pan.
- In a small bowl, combine flour and baking soda.
- In a small saucepan, combine sugar, butter and water. Bring to a boil over medium heat; remove from heat and stir in 1 cup of chocolate chips and vanilla. Continue stirring until chocolate is melted and mixture is smooth. Transfer mixture to a medium bowl. Cool completely. Stir in eggs 1 at a time, beating well after each addition. Gradually stir in flour mixture until smooth. Stir in remaining chocolate chips and the nuts.
- Pour batter into prepared pan and bake until a toothpick inserted in center comes out clean (25 to 35 minutes).
- Cool completely and cut into squares.

YIELD: 16 SERVINGS

Apple Bread Pudding

2	cups finely chopped peeled Granny Smith apples
½	cup packed light brown sugar
¼	cup apple schnapps
4	cups coarsely crumbled stale biscuits or bread
¼	cup raisins
¼	cup chopped dried apricots
¼	cup dried dates
2	cups half-and-half
3	eggs, slightly beaten
1	tablespoon pure vanilla extract
⅔	cup sugar

- Preheat oven to 375 degrees.
- In small shallow pan, combine apples with brown sugar and schnapps. Bake for 15 minutes or until brown sugar melts and apples are tender.
- Toss apples with crumbled biscuits and dried fruits and place in a well-greased baking pan.
- Combine half-and-half, eggs, vanilla and sugar and pour over bread. Bake for 30 to 45 minutes or until custard is firm and golden brown.
- Serve warm. To serve, cut into squares, place each square in a shallow bowl, top with a scoop of cinnamon ice cream and butterscotch sauce.
- If preparing in advance, refrigerate. Wrap in foil to rewarm, or place individual servings in microwave for a few seconds.

YIELD: 8 SERVINGS

Strawberry Shortcake with Buttermilk Almond Biscuits

This wonderful shortcake was adapted from *Home Desserts* by Richard Sax which is our favorite book of desserts. It's a real favorite with our conference groups. We've even frozen the extra biscuits, just thaw them completely at room temperature.

3	*pints ripe fresh strawberries*
1/4	*to 1/2 cup sugar*
2	*tablespoons Amaretto liqueur (optional)*
2 1/4	*cups all-purpose flour*
1/2	*cup sugar*
1 1/2	*teaspoons baking powder*
3/4	*teaspoon baking soda*
1/4	*teaspoon salt*
6	*tablespoons cold unsalted butter, cut into pieces*
2/3	*cup (or more) buttermilk*
1	*large egg yolk*
1/2	*teaspoon vanilla extract*
1/2	*teaspoon almond extract*
2	*tablespoons heavy cream or milk for glazing biscuits*
1/2	*cup sliced almonds*
1	*tablespoon sugar*
	Ice cream

☙ Wash berries, hull and slice them. Purée 1/3 of the berries with 1/4 cup sugar and Amaretto in food processor or blender, taste and add more sugar if desired. Toss the sliced strawberries with the purée and refrigerate. I like to bring the berries out and let them come to room temperature about an hour before serving.

❧ Preheat oven to 425 degrees. Combine flour, ½ cup sugar, baking powder, baking soda and salt in food processor and pulse briefly to combine. Add butter and pulse briefly until mixture is crumbly. In a small bowl whisk together ⅔ cup buttermilk, egg yolk, vanilla and almond extract. With the processor running, pour this mixture through the food tube into the machine. Turn off the machine. Add more buttermilk a tablespoon at a time if needed, pulsing briefly after each addition until mixture is wet enough to form a slightly sticky but manageable dough.

❧ Turn the dough out onto a floured surface. Sprinkle with a small amount of flour and roll or pat out to ¾-inch thickness. Cut out biscuits with 3-inch biscuit cutter, rerolling scraps as needed but handle as gently as possible. Transfer biscuits to a buttered baking sheet. Brush the tops with cream or milk and scatter the almonds over the biscuits. Sprinkle with 1 tablespoon sugar.

❧ Bake biscuits in 425-degree oven for 10 to 15 minutes or until golden brown. Check after 10 minutes and watch carefully as baking times can vary greatly from one oven to another. Remove from oven. If you want to serve them immediately, let cool for several minutes, then slice each biscuit into halves with a serrated knife, and continue immediately with ice cream and berries as described below. If you don't plan to serve them for 1 to 2 hours, wait until they cool completely before slicing them. They'll be less crumbly.

❧ To assemble shortcakes: If your ice cream is frozen hard, soften it slightly in the refrigerator or at room temperature. Place the bottom half of each biscuit on a serving plate, spoon some of the berries onto the biscuit, then top with a scoop of ice cream, mashing it down slightly. Spoon the rest of the berries over the ice cream and replace the lids of the biscuits at an angle over the ice cream and berries. Garnish with fresh mint and more berries if desired.

YIELD: 6 SERVINGS

Apple Cranberry Napoleon*

7	egg roll wrappers or
	21 won ton wrappers
1/2	teaspoon cinnamon
1/4	cup sugar
6	Granny Smith apples
1	cup dried cranberries —1/8 inch slices
2	cups apple cider
2	teaspoons butter
1	cup packed brown sugar
1	teaspoon vanilla extract

- Preheat oven to 400 degrees.

- Cut egg roll wrappers into 3 equal squares to make 21 squares or use 21 won ton wrappers. (You only need 3 squares for each Napoleon but I always make a few extra in case some of them get too brown in the oven.)

- Place the pastry squares on a cookie sheet that has been sprayed lightly with nonstick spray. Spray tops of squares lightly with nonstick spray also. Combine cinnamon and sugar and sprinkle over squares (a salt shaker is handy for this).

- Bake for 3 to 4 minutes or until lightly browned, watching carefully to see how long it takes in your oven. Once they start to brown, watch continuously as they burn in a few seconds. Set aside to cool.

- Peel and quarter apples. Slice into 1/8-inch circles. slices Place cranberries and cider in a small saucepan and boil cider until it is reduced to about 2/3 cup.

- In a nonstick pan, melt butter and add brown sugar and apple slices. Toss in pan over medium heat until apples are tender and caramelized. Add reduced cider with cranberries and add vanilla. Cook for a few more minutes or until syrupy.

- Set aside at room temperature until just before serving or refrigerate and rewarm just before serving, adding a bit more cider or water if mixture seems dry.

- To assemble: On each dessert plate, place 1 pastry square, top with a spoonful of apples and sauce, repeat with pastry and apples once more and finish with last pastry squares on top. Turn each square at a different angle from the one below it to make a more attractive presentation. Dust top with confectioners' sugar if desired.

YIELD: 6 SERVINGS

Butterscotch Sauce

1/2	cup water
1	pound light brown sugar
1	cup light corn syrup
3	ounces butter
1/4	cup apple schnapps
1/2	cup heavy cream

- In a medium saucepan, combine water, brown sugar, syrup and butter. Cook over low heat until butter melts. Bring to a boil and cook, stirring for 1 minute.
- Remove from heat and add schnapps and cream. Whisk well. Store in refrigerator. Will keep for at least a week.

YIELD: 6 SERVINGS

Chocolate Sauce

1	cup heavy cream
3/4	to 1 cup premium quality semisweet chocolate chips

- Warm cream in a double boiler over low heat. Stir in chips.
- Continue heating and whisking until chips are melted and mixture is smooth.

YIELD: 3 SERVINGS

Bananas Foster

This is a traditional New Year's dessert at Glen-Ella Springs. I put my chafing dish on a rolling cart and go through the dining room serving it tableside. It's very impressive and not difficult, but do be careful.

1/4	*cup butter*
3/4	*cup packed brown sugar*
1/2	*teaspoon cinnamon*
1/2	*vanilla bean or 1/2 teaspoon vanilla extract*
3 1/2	*tablespoons banana liqueur*
2	*tablespoons 151-proof rum for igniting sauce*
	Vanilla ice cream
2	*bananas*
	Wooden kitchen matches
	Long-handled serving spoon

- Melt butter in a saucepan over low heat. Add brown sugar, cinnamon, vanilla bean and banana liqueur. Stir mixture until ingredients are well combined. Watch carefully and do not let mixture boil or it could ignite. Set sauce aside at room temperature until needed.

- To serve tableside in a chafing dish: Make sure your chafing dish pan will get hot enough to flame the sauce, or use a pan on a portable butane burner or just use your stove if it's near enough to your serving area for your guests to watch this presentation. You might want to try flaming the sauce once in advance to avoid having a mess on your hands. I would also advise having a portable fire extinguisher ready in case there's an accident. Alcohol doesn't burn for very long, but it can be dangerous if you aren't careful.

- ❧ Have 151-proof rum ready in a small pitcher. Scoop vanilla ice cream into number of portions needed and place in freezer until just before serving.

- ❧ Rewarm sauce on stove. Remove vanilla bean and discard. Pour sauce into chafer or shallow pan large enough to hold sauce and bananas.

- ❧ Slice bananas lengthwise and then in half to make 8 pieces. Add bananas to sauce in pan or chafing dish.

- ❧ Place ice cream in serving dishes and bring to serving area.

- ❧ Heat pan or chafer just until sauce begins to bubble. Immediately pour rum into sauce but don't stir in. Light a long kitchen match and touch flame to area where you poured the rum. The sauce should ignite. Carefully stir flame through sauce and ladle with bananas over ice cream into each dish.

- ❧ The 151-proof rum for this dish is not essential, but it ignites very quickly—we call it liquid fire. You can use a lower proof rum or liquor but it may not light as easily.

YIELD: 4 SERVINGS

Lemon Balm

Crème Caramel

———— ✺ ————

3/4	cup sugar
3	tablespoons water
1/4	vanilla bean or 1/2 teaspoon
	vanilla extract
1	cup whole milk
1/2	cup heavy cream
2	eggs
1	egg yolk
1/4	cup sugar

➢ Preheat oven to 300 degrees.

➢ Spray 4 ovenproof glass custard cups with baking spray and place them in a shallow baking pan.

➢ To make caramel, put 3/4 cup of sugar in a heavy-bottomed saucepan with 3 tablespoons of water. Bring the sugar mixture to a boil and cook until it begins to caramelize.

➢ The less you "play with" the sugar while it is caramelizing, the better. The best way is just to leave it alone and let it "do its thing" while you watch.

➢ When it starts to change color it will go quickly, so watch it carefully and be prepared to pour it immediately into the custard cups as soon as it reaches the desired caramel color, not too light and not too dark —you may have to try this procedure several times before you get the hang of it.

➢ Pour the caramel into the custard cups while it is still hot.

➢ To make the custard, cut vanilla bean in half and scrape the goo from the center of the bean with the point of a paring knife.

➢ In a saucepan, put the milk, cream, the pod and the goo from the vanilla bean (or just vanilla extract) and scald the milk over medium heat. This means just to heat it briefly.

➢ Retrieve the vanilla bean pod from the milk and discard it. Remove pan from direct heat, but keep warm.

➢ Whisk the eggs and the yolk together and add the 1/4 cup sugar. Pour a small amount of the egg mixture into the milk mixture and stir. Then pour in the rest of the egg mixture and mix well.

•▶ Pour the custard into the cups on top of the caramel, filling them evenly within ¼ inch of the rim. Pour hot water into the pan around the cups to halfway up the sides of the custard cups.

•▶ Cover the pan with foil, leaving 1 corner uncovered to let steam escape. We find this really helps to cook them evenly without over browning.

•▶ Bake for 45 to 60 minutes or until a metal knife inserted in the center comes out clean. Cool and refrigerate.

•▶ To unmold, place custards in a shallow pan of hot water for a couple of minutes to loosen the caramel. Run a sharp knife around the custards and turn them out onto a serving plate. The caramel will run and form a sauce around the custards.

YIELD: 4 SERVINGS

Vanilla or Amaretto Custard Sauce

1	cup heavy cream, half-and-half or milk
2	egg yolks
3	tablespoons sugar
½	teaspoon vanilla extract

•▶ In the top of a double boiler over simmering water, heat cream until hot but not boiling. Beat egg yolks well in a small bowl. Combine a small amount of the hot cream with the egg yolks and then pour the egg mixture back into the cream. Stir in the sugar.

•▶ Cook and stir custard until it is thick enough to coat the back of a spoon. Remove from heat and stir in vanilla. Chill.

•▶ For Amaretto Custard Sauce, use 1 tablespoon Amaretto liqueur for the vanilla.

YIELD: 6 SERVINGS

Peach Blueberry Cobbler

1	quart sliced fresh peaches
½	cup sugar
2	cups fresh or frozen blueberries
1½	tablespoons cornstarch
¾	cup water
1½	tablespoons margarine, melted
1½	tablespoons lemon juice
¼	cup packed brown sugar
1½	cups self-rising flour
½	teaspoon baking powder
¾	cup sugar
½	cup margarine, melted
¾	cup (or more) milk
¼	teaspoon nutmeg
¼	teaspoon allspice
1½	tablespoons sugar

❧ Mix peaches with ½ cup sugar in a bowl and let stand for 1 hour or more. Add the blueberries.

❧ Combine cornstarch, water, 1½ tablespoons margarine, lemon juice and brown sugar and add to fruit. Spread evenly in an 8x8-inch baking pan. *2 quart*

❧ Combine flour, baking powder, ¾ cup sugar, ½ cup margarine and milk in a bowl. Add more milk if needed to make a thick but pourable batter. Spoon evenly over fruit mixture.

❧ Mix nutmeg, allspice and 1½ tablespoons sugar together and sprinkle evenly over batter.

❧ Bake at 325 degrees for 45 minutes or more or until cobbler is bubbling and topping is cooked through. Stick a knife in center of topping to be sure it is done. Serve warm with whipped cream or ice cream.

YIELD: 12 SERVINGS

Apple Sour Cream Streusel Pie

1½	cups all-purpose flour
½	cup sugar
1	teaspoon baking powder
4	ounces butter
1	egg
1	tablespoon apple schnapps
¼	cup sugar
1	tablespoon all-purpose flour
2	eggs
¾	cup sour cream
½	teaspoon cinnamon
¾	teaspoon vanilla extract
¼	teaspoon lemon zest
¼	teaspoon freshly grated nutmeg
	Dash of salt
2	cups sliced peeled tart apples
3	tablespoons sugar
2	tablespoons brown sugar
¼	cup all-purpose flour
1	teaspoon cinnamon
2	ounces cold butter
¼	cup chopped walnuts

🍂 Combine 1½ cups flour, ½ cup sugar, baking powder, 4 ounces butter, 1 egg and apple schnapps in food processor. Process until ingredients are just combined; press into greased 9-inch pie pan. Blend ¼ cup sugar, 1 tablespoon flour and 2 eggs. Whisk in sour cream, ½ teaspoon cinnamon, vanilla, lemon zest, nutmeg and salt. Fold in apples. Turn into pie shell and bake at 350 degrees for 30 minutes.

🍂 Combine 3 tablespoons sugar, brown sugar, ¼ cup flour, 1 teaspoon cinnamon, 2 ounces butter and walnuts in food processor; process until crumbly.

🍂 Take pie from oven and sprinkle with streusel topping and bake for 30 minutes more. Cool to room temperature before serving.

YIELD: 8 SERVINGS

Fruit Tart with Pecan Crust

This recipe came from Glen Powel who was in charge of menu and recipe development for the Peasant Restaurants for many years, and now has Agnes and Muriel's Restaurant in Atlanta. We love to serve this on a buffet table. It makes a beautiful presentation and is also delicious. Let guests help themselves or have someone cut and serve the tart from the buffet table.

1	pound flour
1/4	cup sugar
1/2	teaspoon salt
1/2	pound cold butter
2	eggs, slightly beaten
2	tablespoons water
1/2	pound pecans, toasted, finely ground
2	tablespoons egg whites, beaten slightly
1/4	cup sugar
2	pounds cream cheese, softened
1	cup sugar
2	tablespoons Amaretto liqueur
	(or substitute 1 teaspoon vanilla
	extract for liqueur)
	Strawberries, kiwifruit, bananas,
	blueberries, blackberries, etc.
	Apple jelly for glaze

- Combine flour, 1/4 cup sugar and salt in mixer bowl. Cut butter into small pieces and blend with flour on slow speed until mixture resembles coarse crumbs.

- Combine eggs and water and add to mixer bowl. Add toasted pecans and mix until a dough forms. Divide dough into 2 equal-size flat rounds, cover well with plastic wrap and refrigerate for at least 1 hour.

🍓 Roll out dough into desired shape about ⅛ inch thick, pinching off and patching where needed. This does not have to be neat because you will cover the whole thing with cream cheese and fruit. You can make a rectangle, square or circle, or make more than 1, or freeze 1 piece for later use. Transfer carefully to a flat baking sheet large enough to fit, or bake in more than 1 piece and fit together after baking. Brush with egg whites and sprinkle with ¼ cup sugar.

🍓 Bake at 350 degrees for 20 minutes or until golden brown. Remove from oven and let cool. The cooked crust will crumble easily, so handle it as little as possible.

🍓 Blend softened cream cheese, 1 cup sugar and Amaretto and set aside. Refrigerate if not using that day, but bring to room temperature before spreading on crust.

🍓 Spread filling on cooled crust covering completely about ⅛ inch thick.

🍓 Slice large fruit such as strawberries, kiwifruit and bananas. (Don't slice bananas in advance as they will turn dark fairly quickly.) Leave small berries whole; blackberries can be halved if they are large. Arrange fruit attractively in alternating rows over cream cheese, keeping rows as close together as possible. Melt apple jelly and brush lightly over fruit. This prevents bananas from turning and glazes the fruit. Refrigerate if not serving immediately.

YIELD: 25 SERVINGS

Strawberry

Pecan Pie

—⟨∘∘∘⟩—

1/3   *cup margarine*
1   *cup corn syrup*
2/3   *cup sugar*
3   *eggs*
1   *teaspoon vanilla extract*
1   *cup coarsely chopped pecans*
1   *(9-inch) unbaked pie shell*

❧ Melt margarine and combine with corn syrup, sugar, eggs and vanilla. Stir in coarsely chopped pecans.

❧ Pour into unbaked 9-inch pie shell and bake at 350 degrees until set (about 1 hour).

❧ You may need to cover edge of shell with foil to keep from browning too much.

YIELD: 8 SERVINGS

Mint

Fresh Pumpkin Pie

For years we used canned pumpkin for our pumpkin pies at Thanksgiving. Then one year an employee brought me a pie made with fresh pumpkin and I'll never be happy with the canned stuff again. There's a world of difference to me. This is a basic recipe that probably came straight from one of our basic cookbooks — I can't remember which one, but it's good.

1	fresh pumpkin at least 1½ to 2 pounds
1	cup sugar
½	teaspoon salt
1½	teaspoons cinnamon
½	teaspoon ground ginger
½	teaspoon ground cloves
1½	cups evaporated milk
½	cup milk
2	eggs, slightly beaten
1	(9-inch) unbaked pie shell

➢ The best way to cook pumpkin is to steam it. Cut the pumpkin into large chunks, removing as much of the center fibrous part as you can but without peeling it. You can bake the pumpkin seeds separately for a crunchy snack.

➢ Place the pumpkin pieces on a steamer rack over boiling water in a large pot and steam for 30 to 45 minutes or until the flesh is tender. Cool and scrape or cut the pumpkin meat away from the skin. Purée enough pumpkin to have 1½ cups purée for the pie. Use any extra to make pumpkin bread or freeze it.

➢ Preheat oven to 425 degrees.

➢ Combine sugar, salt, cinnamon, ginger, cloves, evaporated milk, milk and eggs in a large bowl and beat until smooth. Stir in the pumpkin purée. Pour into pie shell.

➢ Bake for 10 minutes, then reduce oven temperature to 300 degrees and bake for about 45 minutes or until firm.

YIELD: 8 SERVINGS

Frozen Cappuccino Soufflés

A great make-ahead party dessert. A lovely end for an elegant party. Refreshing and impressive.

> 1¼ cups sugar
> ½ cup water
> 4 eggs
> 4 egg yolks
> ½ cup coffee liqueur
> 3 cups heavy cream
> 2 teaspoons espresso or other finely
>   ground coffee
>   Chocolate Sauce (page 155)

⟫ Take 8 ovenproof glass baking dishes and make a 2-inch foil collar for each 1 with a triple thickness of foil long enough to wrap around the dish with 1 inch or so overlap. Wrap the collars around the dishes so they stick up at least 1 inch past the rim, and secure with masking tape.

⟫ Combine sugar and water. Bring to a boil for 5 to 8 minutes or until mixture reaches the soft-boil stage or 238 degrees on a candy thermometer.

⟫ Meanwhile, in a mixer on high speed, beat eggs and egg yolks for 10 minutes or until pale yellow. Reduce mixer speed to low and pour hot sugar syrup into eggs in a thin stream.

⟫ Add liqueur and continue beating until completely cool.

⟫ Whip cream until firm. Fold espresso and ⅓ of the cream at a time into cool mixture and mix until completely smooth. Spoon evenly into soufflé dishes and freeze until firm. To serve, remove foil collar and turn out of dishes onto serving plates which have been ladled with warm Chocolate Sauce. Dust with powdered cocoa if desired.

YIELD: 8 SERVINGS

Cinnamon Ice Cream

—⚬⚬⚬—

½   gallon vanilla ice cream
     (premium brand), softened
1   tablespoon ground cinnamon
3   tablespoons sugar
2   tablespoons apple schnapps

❧ Place ice cream in large bowl of mixer and beat on low speed until softened. Add other ingredients. Mix to combine thoroughly and refreeze.

YIELD: 8 SERVINGS

Fig Ice Cream

—⚬⚬⚬—

Wonderful stuff! If you have a fig tree or if you're a lover of fresh figs, don't fail to try it.

½   gallon vanilla ice cream
2   cups puréed fresh figs
¼   cup dark rum (optional)

❧ Soften ice cream and place in large bowl of mixer. Add other ingredients and mix until thoroughly combined. Pour into a container and refreeze.

YIELD: 8 SERVINGS

Fresh Strawberry Sherbet*

This recipe is such an easy and flavorful dessert to prepare, and with no fat. The amount of sugar can be reduced by ½ to 1 cup if the strawberries are very ripe and sweet.

2½	quarts fresh strawberries
3½	cups sugar
5	tablespoons fresh lemon juice
2	cups plain nonfat yogurt

- Wash, stem and slice strawberries. Mix with sugar and lemon juice and set aside for 1 hour or more.
- Add yogurt and process in food processor until smooth. Freeze in 1-gallon ice cream churn.

YIELD: 16 SERVINGS

Strawberry

Ice Cream Fantasy

———◦◦◦———

A yummy ice cream cake. I made this at the Peasant Uptown when I worked there, but I like our flavor combinations better.

1	*cup vanilla wafer crumbs*
1/3	*cup chopped pecans*
1½	*ounces margarine, melted*
½	*gallon chocolate ice cream*
½	*gallon butter pecan ice cream*
2	*cups coffee ice cream*
1	*cup chopped toasted pecans*

➢ Combine vanilla wafer crumbs, ⅓ cup chopped pecans and margarine. Press over bottom of greased 9- or 10-inch springform pan. Bake at 325 degrees for 5 minutes in convection oven. Freeze before filling.

➢ Soften ice creams in refrigerator or at room temperature. Wearing rubber gloves helps keep your hands from freezing.

➢ Mold chocolate ice cream around edge of springform pan. Continue with butter pecan, then coffee ice cream in the center. Top with 1 cup chopped pecans.

➢ Freeze until firm. When ready to serve, dip pan briefly in warm water to release ice cream from sides of pan. Unmold and slice into 8 to 10 wedges with a sharp knife. Run knife blade under hot water to help in slicing. Serve with warm Butterscotch Sauce (page 155) drizzled over the top.

YIELD: 8 TO 10 SERVINGS

Nutritional Profile Guidelines

The editors have attempted to present these recipes in a form that allows approximate nutritional values to be computed. Persons with dietary or health problems or whose diets require close monitoring should not rely solely on the nutritional information provided. They should consult their physicians or a registered dietitian for specific information.

Abbreviations for Nutritional Profile

Cal—Calories	Fiber—Dietary Fiber	Sod—Sodium
Prot—Protein	T Fat—Total Fat	g—grams
Carbo—Carbohydrates	Chol—Cholesterol	mg—milligrams

Nutritional information for these recipes is computed from many sources, including materials supplied by the United States Department of Agriculture, computer databanks, and journals in which the information is assumed to be in the public domain. However, many specialty items, new products, and processed foods may not be available from these sources or may vary from the average values used in these profiles. More information on new and/or specific products may be obtained by nutrient labels. Unless otherwise specified, the nutritional profile of these recipes is based on all measurements being level.

➣ **Alcoholic ingredients** have been analyzed for the basic ingredients, although cooking causes the evaporation of alcohol, thus decreasing caloric content.

➣ **Eggs** are all large. To avoid raw eggs that may carry salmonella, use an equivalent amount of pasteurized egg substitute.

➣ **Flour** is unsifted all-purpose flour.

➣ **Garnishes**, serving suggestions, and other additions and variations are not included in the profile.

➣ **Margarine** and **butter** are regular, not whipped or presoftened.

➣ **Milk** is whole milk, 3.5% butterfat. Lowfat milk is 1% butterfat. Evaporated milk is whole milk with 60% of the water removed.

➣ **Oil** is any type of vegetable cooking oil. **Shortening** is hydrogenated vegetable shortening.

➣ **Salt** and other ingredients to taste as noted in the ingredients have not been included in the nutritional profile.

➣ If a choice of ingredients has been given, the nutritional profile reflects the first option. If a choice of amounts has been given, the nutritional profile reflects the greater amount.

Nutritional Profiles

Pg #	Recipe Title (Approx Per Serving)	Cal	Prot (g)	Carbo (g)	T Fat (g)	Chol (mg)	Fiber (g)	Sod (mg)
21	Black-Eyed Pea Salsa	56	4	10	<1	0	2	310
23	Yogurt Cheese and Herbed Yogurt Cheese	24	2	4	0	1	<1	38
38	Salmon Cured with Tequila and Herbs*	225	26	16	4	60	2	2542
49	Red Bell Pepper and Tomato Soup	114	5	17	3	<1	4	531
52	Bibb Lettuce Salad with Cranberry Vinaigrette	179	2	32	5	0	3	23
54	Kidney Bean Salad	219	8	37	5	0	6	534
58	Cucumbers and Onion	34	1	8	<1	0	2	484
64	Pasta Salad with Wild Mushrooms and Olives	588	17	67	29	25	6	544
66	Honey Dijon Vinaigrette	89	<1	6	7	0	<1	127
75	Lemon Poppy Seed Muffins	136	4	26	2	21	2	311
79	Date Nut Prune Bread	264	5	41	11	35	3	267
98	Marinated Asparagus	209	5	12	18	0	4	76
100	Oven-Roasted Beets with Balsamic Vinaigrette	286	1	6	29	0	1	56
104	Broiled Radicchio with Balsamic Vinegar	41	1	2	4	0	<1	8
108	Broiled Tomatoes	368	21	12	27	54	1	1151
121	Salmon in Parchment	378	33	3	25	133	1	197
123	Grilled Tuna with Orange Ginger Sauce	460	41	7	29	67	<1	100
136	Summer Supper Pasta	518	25	73	14	103	7	510
154	Apple Cranberry Napoleon	452	4	107	3	6	5	214
168	Fresh Strawberry Sherbet	209	2	52	<1	1	2	20

*Nutritional information includes the entire amount of kosher salt.

Index

Order Information

Glen-Ella Springs Inn, Inc.

1789 Bear Gap Road
Clarkesville, GA 30523

———

Phone
(706) 754-7295

Fax
(706) 754-1560

Email
info@glenella.com

	Qty	Total
Glen-Ella Springs Recipes and Remembrances $19.95 each		
Georgia residents add 6% sales tax $1.20 each		
Postage and Handling $3.00 each		
Gift Wrap $1.60 each		
Total		

Ship to:

Name _____

Street Address _____

City _____ State _____ Zip _____

Daytime Phone (   ) _____ Nighttime Phone (   ) _____

Send Gift Card:

To _____

From _____

Message _____

Method of Payment: ☐ American Express   ☐ MasterCard

        ☐ VISA   ☐ Check or Money Order

Card Number _____ Expiration Date _____

Signature _____

Please make checks payable to Glen-Ella Springs Inn, Inc.